M000159469

LIFE
LESSONS

LIFE
LESSONS

Wisdom and Wit from
Life's Ups and Downs

JAY BLADES

with Ian Gittins

bluebird
books for life

First published 2023 by Bluebird
an imprint of Pan Macmillan
The Smithson, 6 Briset Street, London EC1M 5NR
EU representative: Macmillan Publishers Ireland Ltd, 1st Floor,
The Liffey Trust Centre, 117–126 Sheriff Street Upper,
Dublin 1, D01 YC43
Associated companies throughout the world
www.panmacmillan.com

HB ISBN 978-1-0350-1011-0

Copyright © Jay Blades 2023

The right of Jay Blades to be identified as the
author of this work has been asserted by him in accordance
with the Copyright, Designs and Patents Act 1988.

All rights reserved. No part of this publication may be reproduced,
stored in a retrieval system, or transmitted, in any form, or by any means
(electronic, mechanical, photocopying, recording or otherwise)
without the prior written permission of the publisher.

Pan Macmillan does not have any control over, or any responsibility for,
any author or third-party websites referred to in or on this book.

1 3 5 7 9 8 6 4 2

A CIP catalogue record for this book is available from the British Library.

Typeset in Fournier MT Std by Palimpsest Book Production Ltd, Falkirk, Stirlingshire

Printed and bound by CPI Group (UK) Ltd, Croydon, CR0 4YY

This book is sold subject to the condition that it shall not, by way of
trade or otherwise, be lent, hired out, or otherwise circulated without
the publisher's prior consent in any form of binding or cover other than
that in which it is published and without a similar condition including
this condition being imposed on the subsequent purchaser.

Visit **www.panmacmillan.com/bluebird** to read more about all our books
and to buy them. You will also find features, author interviews and
news of any author events, and you can sign up for e-newsletters
so that you're always first to hear about our new releases.

CONTENTS

INTRODUCTION

'Life Lessons?
What's all that *about, then?'*

I think I should begin by addressing this very pertinent question. In fact, it's probably already occurred to you, if you're standing flicking through this volume in a bookshop or browsing online. *Life Lessons?* What's all *that* about, then? And why does Jay Blades, off the telly, feel he is qualified or entitled to start dishing them out?

Luckily, I've got a very good answer to this question. It's really quite simple. Life lessons are the tips that you pick up each day as you make your way through this world. They're what you learn from your mistakes, to stop you making the same mistakes again. And they are invaluable. *Gold dust!*

1

Everybody makes mistakes. I'll hold my hands up: anybody who has read my life story, *Making It*, knows I've got a fair few under my belt! Well, the trick is not to let them get you down, or hold you back, but to dust yourself down, learn the life lesson and move on. *Educate yourself.* Because that's what it's all about.

I never got much education in school but I've been learning ever since. For me, a day that you don't learn something is a wasted day. There are lessons all around you, everywhere you go: about people, society and, most of all, yourself. All you need to do is learn to take note and reflect. You can pick up so much.

Another way to describe life lessons might be *positive thinking*. As I see it, it is totally crucial for your sense of self and well-being. If you wake up in the morning and think, 'This is going to be a bad day!', you know what? It almost certainly will be! That's why I realized, long ago, you need a bit of positive thinking to start your day off.

Ten years ago, a long time before I did *The Repair Shop* and before anyone had heard of me, I used to be a community worker. With my ex-wife, Jade, I worked with kids who were on the verge of being excluded from school. I taught these sometimes-troubled teens how to restore furniture in a project that we called Out of the Dark.

Yet furniture restoration wasn't the point. What we were really teaching them was how to feel useful and respect themselves.

Even that early in life, these youths had been written off: by teachers, by friends or even by themselves. They all needed a little push and a bit of encouragement to get themselves back on the right path and going in the right direction.

These kids needed focus, and I realized that one way to give it to them was to start each day in the Out of the Dark workshop with a thought for the day. So, I'd come up with something inspirational and optimistic. We'd talk about it when we all came in in the morning, and we'd keep it with us throughout the day.

One day it might be, 'Walk like you have somewhere to go.' Another it could be, 'The sun won't shine until you put your umbrella away!' These thoughts were just little nuggets, really, pearls of wisdom to make the young people think a bit and give some extra shape and purpose to their day.

I suppose they were my little life lessons, and you know what? Fifteen years on, I'm still dishing them out and, somehow, there are a lot more people listening to them! The credit – or blame?! – for that goes to the internet. It has changed the world, for better and worse, and one of the effects has been to bring my words of wisdom to a bigger audience.

I'll be honest: I can't say I like everything about social media. There's too much negativity on there and I stay well away from that: I just don't need it in my life, thank you very much! But, used right, it can also be a place to spread a bit of love and positive vibes, which is what I try to do.

I put all sorts of stuff up on my socials – news of what I've been up to, pics from *The Repair Shop* – but my favourite things are my thoughts for the day. I don't do them every day – I prefer quality to quantity! – but when I do, I like the thoughts to matter. To *mean* something.

They're short and simple statements but I hope they're profound, in their own way. I hope they have depth. I might say, 'Everything has beauty, but not everyone sees it.' Or, 'No one wins at chess by only moving forward.' I apply the same criteria as I did at Out of the Dark: little snippets to make you *think*.

Me being me, I love turning what I've learned about life into these punchy little sayings and aphorisms – and before you know it, you've got this book! *Bosh!* So, here are my pearls of wisdom. I hope at least some of them can be as useful, and as positive an influence, for you as they've been for me.

You can keep learning, and improving yourself and your sense of well-being, every day of your life until you topple into the grave and start pushing up the daisies. I've made mistakes, sure, but I don't like talking about mistakes, or setbacks: I like to see them as chances to learn and to move on. Like I say, positive thinking!

So, are you ready to learn a few *Life Lessons*? Good, let's get cracking! And let's start with one of the most important of the lot: don't let yourself, and your life, be limited by where you come from – even if it happens to be humble beginnings.

1

ROOTS

*'Stay on top of your past, so you
can have a better view of your future'*

All of us come from somewhere. Where that is, is beyond our
control. The place and the circumstances that we find ourselves
in are an accident of birth. And there is no doubt that where
we are from shapes us . . . but we shouldn't let it *define* us.

For me, I've got to say, this is one of the most basic and
important life lessons of all. It's too easy to let where we are
born, and our roots, limit us and lead to us setting low expect-
ations for our lives. Well, it might be easy but it is also a big
mistake. Your past shouldn't be a cage, it should be a springboard.

When I wrote those words on social media: 'Stay on top of
your past, so you can have a better view of your future', what

I was getting at was that you stay on top of your past by being *proud* of it. And being proud of your past can take you to another level. When you own where, and what, you came from, it elevates you.

'Stay on top of your past, so you can have a better view of your future.'

I know it's easier said than done. I understand that some people are ashamed of their roots, and I get that. At the same time, it makes no sense: why be ashamed of something that's not your fault and wasn't your choice? The only way forward is to own it and embrace it. Squeeze those lemons and make some lemonade!

I mean, let's look at me. Some people might say that I had a very disadvantaged beginning in life. As it happens, I don't particularly agree with them, but let's just look at my initial circumstances:

- I'm from Hackney, in East London. It's very trendy now, *darling*, but back in the day, a lot of people thought it was a proper ghetto.
- I was a little Black kid in an era when racism was a lot more obvious and in-your-face every day than it is now.
- My mum was only eighteen when she had me. She did her best, and I love her to bits, but there was a whole lot she didn't know about being a parent.

- My dad didn't want to know. He wasn't around. In fact, anyone who has read my life story, *Making It*, knows that I don't even like calling him my dad: I prefer to say The Man Who Contributed Towards My Birth, or TMWCTMB.

- I have chronic dyslexia. I wasn't diagnosed until I was thirty and so as a kid, I was just written off as stupid. This limited my life options for a very long time.

So, it wasn't quite what you'd call a dream start in life, was it? But here's another saying that I shared on my socials a while back, another life lesson: 'Where I'm from, we had three choices in life: Give up, give in, or give it all you've got.' And I know which one *I* was always going to choose.

There is no doubt about it: in Hackney, back in the seventies and eighties, you were always up against it. It wasn't the sort of place where you could go out and go skipping happily down the street. There was always trouble around in some shape or form and it would usually find you, whether you wanted it or not.

'Where I'm from, we had three choices in life: Give up, give in, or give it all you've got.'

I'll give you a for-instance. A lot of people were shocked when I talked in *Making It* about going through police brutality as a youth. I guess some *Repair Shop* viewers, raised in comfy, leafy, middle-class suburbs, might find it impossible to believe that cops might give a young Black guy a kicking just for the colour of his skin. Well, I'm sorry to report, that was what used to happen. That was how life was!

I'll never forget – even nearly forty years on – being pulled from the street into a parked van full of cops. As soon as you saw the eager looks in their eyes, you'd know what was about to happen, and you couldn't do jack-shit about it.

They were nasty, but they weren't stupid. They'd stick wet towels on you, to prevent any tell-tale bruising, get their truncheons out, and beat the crap out of you. I'd be curled into a ball on the floor of the van as the blows and kicks came raining in. It hurt like hell, and it wasn't just me. It happened to all my mates.

No wonder we hated the police! No wonder we thought of them as pigs! Yet you can't go through life scarred by stuff like that. You can't carry grudges for ever. If I'd carried on all through my days going 'I hate the police!', I'd never have been able to move on and improve myself. I'd have been stuck: brooding, damaged and emotionally scarred.

The funny thing is that, when I went to university in my thirties, I actually ended up working with the police! A Chief Superintendent, David McWhirter, heard that I was doing community work and asked me to organize local youths to talk to his officers to tell them exactly what they were doing wrong.

I have to tell you, that took some believing – *Me! Training the police!* But it was a great exercise and it ended up doing a lot of good. It was a real benefit to the kids and the community, and I would not have been able to do it if I'd still been living in the past and hating all cops for what some of them used to do to me.

I mean, I hadn't forgotten their violence and abuse – how could I? – but it was a classic example of what I'm talking about here. A perfect encapsulation of the life lesson that I'm trying to explain: *stay on top of your past, so you can have a better view of your future.*

Mind you, it's important not to take that saying the wrong way. You could mis-interpret 'Stay on top of your past' as 'Stand on the people that you came from, because they are below you now.' Nothing could be further from the truth. I'm saying, 'Those people are your grounding in your life. They're your foundation.'

The strange thing is, I didn't actually feel disadvantaged when I was growing up in Hackney. As a kid, you just know what you know. It was only when I got older and started applying for jobs that I realized: *Oh! The colour of my skin is a problem for some people! And the place where I grew up is too.*

It's only with hindsight that you fully understand what you came from. Now, I look back and see that a lot of people gave up on life way too early. They went off into criminality – selling drugs, prostitution, whatever – because that was what they saw around them. They figured that was their fate and they had no alternative. I'm not being hard on those people, or coming down on them. They copied what was going on locally and they genuinely believed that selling drugs, or walking the streets, was their route to getting on. It was their way of believing they were controlling their life situations – except, of course, that they really weren't.

I sometimes wonder why I didn't fall into that trap myself. I have to admit, I came close at times. It took an arrest, and a conviction for possession, to bring me to my senses on that one. If I am honest, I think the main reason I never went too far down that particular dead-end was that, even as a kid, I had an insane amount of confidence. Without being funny, I always felt that I might do big things. I just never knew what they would be!

Was it confidence, or was it naivety, that meant I just wouldn't accept the limitations my roots seemed to have given me? I'm not sure. Probably a bit of both. I just know I always wanted to push into new, different environments and try to achieve things when I got there. Nowhere ever felt out of bounds to me.

And, you know what? If I can do it, *anyone* can! You may be shaking your head as you read this, or thinking, *I ain't got your front, Jay!* – but that's my point! Even if you come from humble surroundings, you can still have that 'Never give up!' spirit. I feel grateful that I do, and I think it was Hackney that gave it to me.

What do I mean? Again, look at me! I'm not an obvious geezer to have got to a point where I'm hosting TV shows, writing books and working with His Royal Highness King Charles III! Nobody would have looked at the fourteen-year-old Jay Blades and said, 'Yep, he'll be a TV presenter!' And I never would've been without a lot of positive thinking.

The main part of that positive thinking was simply *not giving up on life*. Because I was never going to do that. Even leaving school with no qualifications at all – and I mean diddly-squat! – I was never going to sign on the dole and sit doing nothing. That equals not participating in life. And *I like to participate*.

I've never liked lying in bed. I've always woken up and wanted to jump up and *do* something. That was as true of me at sixteen, when I was casting around for who I was, as it is today. And the good thing is that, even in what might be seen as unpromising circumstances, you can *always* find something to do.

When I was sixteen, I learned there was an agency – well, basically a geezer on a street corner, with a piece of paper in his hand – who would dish out cash-in-hand work each day to unqualified lads like me. All you had to do was show up at six o'clock in the morning, look eager and hope for the best.

I didn't always get lucky. I remember one week, I walked two miles there from my estate at the crack of dawn every single day and didn't get even one job. The guy just ignored me every day! Walking back home rejected, in the rain, was proper demoralizing, but I knew the important thing was to stay motivated. And to go back the next morning.

When the bloke *did* start choosing me, he sent me to some right dodgy gaffs – sausage factories. Messy storage lockups. Building sites. But it taught me how to graft, gave me some experience, and put some wedge in my back pocket for the weekend. And at that age, that was what I wanted.

I reckon there're a few decent morals to this tale, a few life lessons. Show up on time, even if it's six in the morning. Stay motivated. And don't think any work is beneath you, because it's (nearly) always better than doing zilch. And the chances are it might teach you something useful about yourself.

What it taught *me*, I think, is that I'm a bit of an entrepreneur. I always want to make things happen. And maybe, in a way, that is a good consequence of being from a 'disadvantaged' background. You learn to live on your wits and make things happen, because nobody else is going to do it for you.

Never be ashamed of your background! Celebrate it, because that shows other people from those places that they can achieve as well. There is a stereotyped idea: 'Oh, you have to come from a good area, and a good family, to do anything in life.' And it's Just. Not. True. Many, many people with unpromising roots have achieved miracles.

I want to hit you with another favourite saying: 'A successful person is someone who can lay a firm foundation with bricks that others throw at them.' And I think this is a saying that everyone should burn into their brains, because it is proper, proper important.

I mean, I've had loads of bricks thrown at me over the years! A dad who couldn't be arsed with his own son; the racists who hated me and beat me up because of my skin colour; the teachers and careers advisers who told me I'd amount to nothing. They tried to hold me back, but I used their negativity as rocket fuel: *I'll show you!*

So, here's my next tip: when people chuck those bricks at you, don't put them in your rucksack and carry them around all day. Don't get weighed down by them. What's the point? If you can, do what I always tried to do, and I still do: build something new with the bricks and stand on them. *Build a platform.*

'A successful person is someone who can lay a firm foundation with bricks that others throw at them.'

It's no good blaming people, or situations, that might hold you back. For me, it's like crying over spilt milk. It's not worth it. I don't want to blame my start in life for anything at all. I don't even want to blame The Man Who Contributed Towards My Birth for not being there for me, because that is a dangerous way of thinking.

Why? Well, as soon as you start dishing out blame for your situation to someone, or something else, you are giving yourself an excuse to fail. You are giving yourself a reason not to move on and move forward. And, believe me, you must *never* let anyone tell you that you can't move forward. Just put your head down and *go!*

I stay on top of my past by being proud of where I came from and it can make me protective towards my roots – especially when 'experts' sound off without having a Scooby what they're on about. That happened to me when I went off to study, at thirty years old, at Buckinghamshire New University.

I loved doing my Criminology and Philosophy degree there, and studying changed my life, as I'll talk about later in this book. But some of the lecturers there seemed to have quite stereotypical and even prejudiced attitudes towards my neck of the woods without ever witnessing for themselves what it is actually like.

These professors would hold forth in lectures and tutorials about council estates in the East End of London and they'd make them sound like lawless wastelands. I'd sit in seminars and listen to them describe manors like mine as if they were no more than dysfunctional breeding grounds for crime. *Well, bollocks to that!*

'Unless you have seen it with your eyes, don't talk it with your mouth.'

There is another saying that I like, and that you can learn a lot from: 'Unless you have seen it with your eyes, don't talk it with your mouth.' Because these clever academics had never seen the Pembury Estate in Hackney, or the Packington in Islington, first-hand. Their 'knowledge' of them was totally theoretical.

What they missed, when they talked about them, was the sense of community, friendship, support and belonging you can get on those estates. The camaraderie. *The love.* Their assumptions rubbed me up the wrong way because they didn't know what goes on there. They were guessing.

'I'm not what I've done, I'm what I've overcome.'

Hackney might have been well poor back in the day, but it made me what I am, and I had a lot – a serious lot – of good times there. When you're starting off low down the ladder of society – *give up, give in, or give it all you've got!* – it can inspire you to strive super-hard to better yourself. To climb that ladder.

I think the crux of what I'm trying to say here is in another of my favourite little sayings, which is this: 'I'm not what I've done, I'm what I've overcome.' It's a phrase that acknowledges that anything you achieve in the race of life can feel a lot sweeter if you began that race way behind the starting line.

'What have you overcome then, Jay?' you might ask me. Well, as I've already said, there was my dyslexia. I mean, just think about trying to get through the day without being able to read. It's not easy! As I'll explain, I've not *cured* my dyslexia, because that's not possible, but I've managed to find a way to navigate through it.

I've overcome racism, or rather, my attitude towards racism. Back in the day, if anyone made a racist remark to me, my response was to punch them in the face. It wasn't healthy for anyone, including me. Now I've learned to observe racism, identify it and, if necessary, report it. I've learned not to get violent.

It seems to me that, ultimately, the only way to overcome major hurdles is to see the positive aspects to them. You might think it's hard to see a positive side to poverty or dyslexia or racism, but they've all taught me something. Toughened me up. Even, yeah, given me a few life lessons.

You know what? There's a lot of gentrification in areas like Hackney now, but I sometimes look at the news and I wonder if growing up in my particular bit of the manor may be even harder now than it was back in my day. Humanity is supposed to progress, but I sometimes wonder if we are going backwards.

I mean, my mum never had a lot of money but she always put food on the table for me and my brother, Justin. She didn't have to worry about the cost of putting the radiators on to keep us warm. There wasn't the choice of heating-or-eating that so many people have to make now.

It really saddens me when I look at Hackney now, or at areas like it, and I see food banks everywhere. *Food banks?! What's that all about?* We're living in the twenty-first century, we're in a First World country, and in this modern day, the fastest growing charity sector is food banks? *Wow!*

How can it be that people can't afford to feed themselves, and none of the political parties seem to feel it is an important enough issue to sort out?! There are a lot of people and a lot of charities doing very good work, and helping people, in those areas, but I ask you . . . *food banks*? They just shouldn't need to be there, man!

It upsets me so much because I see it making what is already a hard life for people born into those circumstances so much harder. I mean, how do you stay on top of your past – *or* your present – and make a better future if you are too hungry even to think straight? Or too worried about feeding your family properly? I wonder if kids today have it even harder than I did.

I think what poor areas need right now is an advocate or an ambassador to really champion them. The government needs to be told, 'You have to do a lot more to help these people because, right now, you are really letting them down.' The people in charge of us need to learn some serious life lessons themselves.

I know you have to stay on top of your circumstances to get a better view of your future, but I also know that when you're living in hardship and poverty, it can be all-consuming. I remember that so well as a kid. Hackney – your estate – feels like the whole world. You have narrow horizons, and it's all you can see. You view everything through the prism of your 'hood, and it isn't until you come out of it that you realize there's another world outside of what you know. In fact, a lot of worlds.

There are so many different places and different perspectives, and getting to know them can only broaden your mind.

I think that is probably the best tip I could give a young person growing up today in areas like the Hackney or Leyton of my youth: 'You've got to get out.' I don't mean get out and stay out! I mean get out and see how people elsewhere think and function. See some new places. Ideally, get out of your neighbourhood for a while, if that is where you've always lived.

Why? Well, the problem is, if you only ever look through one window, all that you are ever going to see is the same view. And you'll think that's all there is. Imagine if you spend every day looking through a window on your left side, and it's all concrete as far as the eye can see. Somebody might say, 'Oi! Look through the window to your right, and you'll see a beach and the sea and the sun!' At first, you might answer, 'Nah, I just need this view that I know – I'm all right with the concrete.' But then, finally, you *do* turn your head to the right, and whole new views and vistas and possibilities open up.

So yes, *stay on top of your past, so you can have a better view of your future*, but whatever you do, don't try to leave your past behind. It's part of you, it made you and it shaped you, and the streets where you ran as a kid will always have a special pull for you. In a funny way, they'll always feel like home.

Even today, I go back to Hackney as much as I can. I meet up with my old mates as often as possible. It's really important to me. You can't move from an area and just forget that turf, or forget the people who supported you when you needed it. It would be wrong – and why would anyone *want* to do that, anyway?

Every time I go back to Hackney and see my old muckers, it's emotional. Every. Single. Time. They might tell me they're proud of me if they've seen me on TV, but they don't hold back from giving me a few home truths: 'Oi! Jay! What was you doing in that stupid jacket on *The Repair Shop*? You looked a right muppet!'

I love that and, ultimately, I love the past that I had, and the fact I grew up on a council estate in Hackney. I'm grateful that my mum brought me up the way that she brought me up and I'm even grateful that The Man Who Contributed Towards My Birth wasn't around. Because all of that is what made me what I am.

If you'll let me get philosophical here: all experiences benefit you in the end. Even the racist abuse and beatings as a kid helped to shape me. If I hadn't had them, I mightn't have grown my thick skin and found the fighting spirit that have seen me all right. And I might have had a very different life to this one.

I've got to where I am right now by staying on top of my past, and it also enables me to be excited about the future. Which I am, every day. They say tomorrow never comes – well, the good news is that tomorrow *does* come, every day until you die, and I never know what it is going to bring!

I don't know quite how I do it, but every morning I jump

out of bed early and I feel good about the day ahead. *What will it hold?* I remember once asking my ex-wife, Jade, why she thought I always got up so early. And she just laughed and said, 'It's because you're excited about life.'

Bosh! I love that reason, and I hope I can stay this way! And, like I always say, if I can do it, so can you. Believe me: once you're at peace with your past, your future can be so bright that you'll have to wear shades.

2

EDUCATION

'If you are not willing to learn, no one can help you.
If you are willing to learn, no one can stop you'

I have divided this book into ten separate life lessons but I reckon they're very closely intertwined. They all overlap. And for me what the lessons all have in common is that as you go through life, you should always be willing to learn new things. It's the only way to broaden your mind and to grow your experience.

Think about it! If you go around thinking, *Right, I know everything that I need to know, mate!* and you just do the same old stuff day after day, how are you going to develop as a person? If you're not willing to learn as you go along, you will just stagnate. So, keep your eyes open! Use that grey matter!

With the right attitude, you can learn something new every day of your life. Some people think 'education' just means school and college but, for me, that's looking at things all wrong. Every experience that you have should teach you something. I mean it! There is no better classroom, and no better teacher, than *life* itself.

Conventional education isn't for everyone. When I was a kid, it certainly wasn't for me! I got stuck in the 'L's, the lowest stream in a lousy secondary school and I was abandoned by the teachers. I never expected to get anything out of lessons and so, of course, I didn't. All I learned was how to fight bullies in the playground.

I suppose I could be angry at being neglected by the system like that but the weird thing is that I'm *not*. Everything has its place and its purpose. If I hadn't gone through a hard time at school, I might not have turned out the way I have. I might not be on TV and writing this book now. Everything happens when it has to.

That might sound a bit cosmic – *Oi! Are you some sort of hippy, Jay?* – but I think it's true. I didn't pick up whatever life knowledge I have now from school or from teachers. I got it from experience; from getting out into the world and meeting people from different cultures and backgrounds. I got it from *real life*.

One of the best things I ever did when I was younger was volunteer work. I was offered it when I was just out of my teens. My life was going nowhere much. I was single, on the dole and living with a few blokes I didn't really know in temporary accommodation for homeless people. Things were well bleak, to be honest.

A nice geezer, Michael, who was involved with the Church and with charities, made me an offer. He said I could volunteer at a Christian homeless hostel in Oxford, called Cyrenians. I'd be helping the residents. It wouldn't be a paid job but they'd feed and water me and give me a roof over my head. What did I think?

'If you want something you've never had, you'll have to do something you've never done.'

When you analyse this suggestion, what Michael was actually saying was I could go to a part of the country that I'd never been to, and where I knew nobody, to do a job that I knew nothing about, for no money. I can see why a lot of people might turn that particular offer down flat – but that wasn't my reaction at all.

'Sure, sounds great!' I said to him. 'When can I start?'

Why did I do that? It was just my instant, natural reaction: '*Yeah! Why not?*' In this life, I think you have to open yourself up to as many different experiences as possible. Put yourself in situations where you just don't know what's going to happen. Because that's how you learn – about life, and about yourself.

It's like another little saying I'm fond of: 'If you want something you've never had, you'll have to do something you've never done.' I didn't even know *what* I wanted from my life back then, but I intuited that I'd have to get out of my comfort zone in order to find out. So, that's what I did.

I couldn't have made a better move. I loved life at Oxford Cyrenians from the day I got there. To some eyes, it mightn't have looked so blinding. It was a hostel for old guys who were in a right two-and-eight, and well down on their luck. They had no homes, no families – nothing except the clothes they were standing up in.

From a standing start, having never done anything like it before, I had to care for these guys: feed them, clean them, hose them down and de-louse them when they first came in. It may sound grim, but that's the last thing it was. I became proper friends with these blokes and, for the first time in my life, I felt *useful*.

I learned more about life in those first few weeks at Cyrenians than I had in eleven years in school. Mostly, I learned about myself. I learned that I had compassion in me, and kindness. And I learned that I was good for something a whole lot better than fighting and drifting along in a life that was going nowhere.

The really big thing was that I learned that I could *communicate* with people, in a way that was to prove useful – essential – in my later life, when I went on to do community work and then TV presenting. I had a natural empathy with these poor souls that were down at rock bottom, and I longed to help them.

I know one thing: I'd certainly never have learned all those things about myself if I'd just stayed put in Hackney! As I said earlier: sometimes, you need to look out of a different window. I turned my neck to the right, stared at a completely fresh view, and a whole new set of ideas and possibilities suddenly opened up for me. I was meeting people of a kind I'd never met in my life before and learning to live alongside them, get on with them and help them, as much as I could. I think I was learning all the time at Cyrenians – and another good thing was that maybe, just maybe, some people were also learning from me.

What do I mean? Well, the residents were obviously less fortunate than me, but some people there were a lot *more* fortunate. There were some quite hoity-toity fellow volunteers: well-spoken kids, from privileged backgrounds, maybe taking a gap year off before they went to university.

I hadn't met anyone like them before and it's likely, given their comfortable Home Counties upbringings, that I was the first Black kid, from an East End council estate, that any of *them* had ever met. But we got on great, and maybe it helped to change some of their misconceptions about people of colour. Maybe it helped to broaden *their* minds.

So, here's a life tip I'd give to anybody, young *or* old: if you can, go out and do some volunteering. There are so many amazing charities and organizations out there needing assistance. Get to meet people down on their luck, *and* the people looking after them, and talk to them. Talk to everyone! *That's* how you learn.

It's funny, in a way. All through my life, I've often taken

leaps in the dark, leaps of faith, like the one that I took when I went to Oxford Cyrenians. I haven't known what would happen, or if it would work out, but I've said, 'Why not?' and taken a chance anyway. And that was never truer than when I went to university.

In the year 2000, going to university was *not* the most obvious option for me, to say the least! My life was going through a big slump. I was on my Jack Jones after yet another relationship break-up, living in a rented room, slogging my guts out on building sites every day and, all in all, I was not a happy bunny.

And that wasn't the half of it. I'd hated every minute of secondary school, where I'd learned zilch, left without a single GCSE to my name, and had never opened a book since. Why would I? *I couldn't read!* I was thirty years old and undiagnosed as dyslexic. I mean, what bloody business did I have trying to go to college?!

So why did I do it? Well, I knew instinctively that I had to move my life on, and at the time I was sharing a house with Lisa, a school-teacher friend who I knew was proper intelligent. In fact, I asked her one day where she had got her intelligence from. 'University,' she told me. '*You* should do it, Jay.'

Huh? If I am honest, it would never have occurred to me that university could be appropriate for somebody like me. Nobody from my family had ever gone to uni: I can't even think of anyone off my estate who had. My school just tipped the likes of me out to do what I was doing: menial work, factory work, labouring. Given all that, I know a lot of people in my position would have laughed at the suggestion when they heard it and knocked it on the head straight away – but I didn't. The idea was so mad that something about it appealed to me. *OK*, I said to myself, *let's do it! Where do I find this university, then?*

I told the story in *Making It* of what a plonker I first made of myself when I called up Buckinghamshire New University in High Wycombe, where I was living at the time. I just found the number in the phone book and rang them up. 'Hello!' I said, when a woman picked up. 'I want to go to university!'

She gave a friendly laugh and asked me what I wanted to study – and I hadn't got a clue what to answer! I hadn't even thought that far ahead. If I am being totally honest, I didn't even really know what university was, or what happened there. In my bonce, I just thought of it as *a place where I could get intelligence.*

Seriously! I thought university was like *The Wizard of Oz*! You know how, in the story, the wizard gives the lion courage, and the tin man a heart? I assumed I'd just go to uni and be given a bit of paper that said that I was now intelligent. It never even occurred to me that I might have to read a book or two first.

I talked earlier about liking the fact that I'm quite naive as a person. Well, going to university was a *totally* naive decision for me. I threw myself into it without a clue what would happen and how I'd do there. I took a deep breath – *here we go!* – and I went for it. And it was one of the best things I've ever done.

If I can wax philosophical for a sec – *oh, go on then, Jay!* – life is like a big duvet. Imagine getting into a bed with a lovely warm duvet and just putting it over your big toe! What's the point? You have to dive in, wrap it all around you, experience it, make the most of it. It's the only way to get the most out of it.

University was a totally new experience for me and I absolutely loved it. Writing essays was a nightmare, until I got diagnosed with dyslexia, but the lectures and seminars were a revelation to me. They taught me new ways to think and new ways to express myself. Doing a degree in Criminology and Philosophy meant that, suddenly, I was having deep conversations about existence and what it all means. That was a new one on me! Growing up on a Hackney council estate, I hadn't exactly spent too much time or effort debating the meaning of life or the thoughts of Jean-Paul Sartre! Being asked to think about, and talk about, such topics absolutely blew my mind. It challenged my brain in a way that it had never been challenged before, and I was well up for it. I've never been backward in coming forward so I loved joining in the discussions in classes and tutorials. In fact, I was a very keen student!

It turned out that I was only half-right when I assumed that going to university would 'give me intelligence'. It didn't do that: instead, it gave me the chance to realize that I was intelligent *already*. I had just never had the chance before to explore, express or enjoy that intelligence.

The lecturers and students at uni talked in ways that, initially, were alien to me. One day I was in the canteen and I overheard two lads dissecting and analysing a film they'd seen. I was so intrigued and fascinated that I asked them straight out: 'How come you guys can talk about a film like that?'

They told me they were both doing a film-studies module and I was so excited that I enrolled straight on it. I was even more excited that the lecturer giving the course was a Black guy: Dr Martin Patrick. He was so charismatic and articulate that he had a massive impact on me. He was like a guru! I went to Dr Patrick's film module for a year. I didn't have to, because it wasn't even part of my course, but I just loved learning from him. I loved going along every week and feeling my brain expanding. Like I said earlier: if you want something you've never had, you'll have to do something you've never done.

Bosh! I went into Buckinghamshire New University as a building-site labourer without a qualification to my name. I exited it with a 2:1 degree in Criminology and Philosophy! And I was still the same bloke: I'd just learned to organize and communicate my thoughts so much better. I'd learned how to *think*.

Mind you, I guess this new ability – and having a philosophy degree – did change me a bit! It means that I come out with some right pearls of wisdom sometimes. The other day, I was watching *The Chase* with my wife, Lisa, and she pointed out some bloke who works on the show.

'He's the brainiest man in Britain!' Lisa told me.

'Eh? No, he's not!' I answered.

'How do you work that out?' she asked.

'Because they haven't tested everybody,' I said. 'If they'd tested everybody in Britain on a Monday, maybe he might win, but who knows if someone even more intelligent will be born on the Tuesday? So, philosophically, that's an impossible statement to make!'

And, you know what? I'm not sure if that little gem qualifies as a life lesson, but it's certainly not an observation that I'd have made before I went to university!

Right. I want to go back to the sub-title of this chapter now to explain what I want to talk about next: *If you are not willing to learn, no one can help you. If you are willing to learn, no one can stop you.* Sometimes, that can mean trying to learn something so basic that most people don't even give it a second thought.

It can mean learning to read.

I could never read. As a kid in primary school, the teachers would give the class books to read. I'd open mine, gawp at the pages, and the letters and words would dance up and down in front of me. Nothing would keep still for me to focus on. It was all one big blur and I couldn't make head nor tail of it.

Probably because I was ashamed, I never told my teachers I couldn't read. I got good at bluffing and covering my inability up. And when I got to secondary school, the teachers just assumed that I was stupid because I couldn't read or write, stuck me in the lowest stream and ignored me. They wrote me off: 'Ah, forget him!'

I left school at sixteen still in the same boat and I stayed there for the next fifteen years. *Just think about it.* Imagine walking down the street and not being able to read street signs or newspaper headlines. Imagine buying a gadget and not being able to read the instructions. Crazy, right? Well, welcome to my world!

What was it like? It might sound weird, but I got used to it. It was my reality and I had to live with it. When something is all you've ever known, it feels normal to you, and I'd always find ways to figure stuff out. I recognized the shapes of a few important words. I got very good at guessing. Somehow, I muddled through.

It's mental, but I reckon I'd have gone through my whole life like that if I'd never gone to university. That was where the faeces hit the fan. Suddenly, I was supposed to be studying weighty, intense criminology textbooks and writing essays about them. *Uh-oh!* I couldn't even read the books' bloody titles!

There were some situations that even *I* couldn't bluff my way through, and I was lost and flailing. My tutors were impressed at how well I could discuss proper complex topics in tutorials – 'That's really good, Jay!' – so they couldn't understand why my essays and papers were so rubbish. I never even thought of telling them.

I'd have stayed stuck in that black hole, and failed my degree, if it wasn't for Jade. I met my ex-wife at uni and started dating her, and the penny dropped for her the day she walked in on me and saw me hunched over a book, moving my lips as I pointed at the words. 'Jay!' she said. 'You can't read!'

I didn't deny it. To be honest, it was a relief that she finally knew the enormous burden I was labouring under – and it was an even bigger relief when Jade immediately made a few calls and helped me to do something to address the situation. And what happened next changed my life.

I went to see dyslexia specialists in London. They ran various tests on me: getting me to try to read with one eye covered, and then the other, and through coloured filters. I was pretty crap. Then they put their heads together, had a bit of a chinwag, and gave me their diagnosis.

'Mr Blades,' the kindly woman in charge said. 'You have extreme dyslexia. In fact, you have the approximate reading age of an eleven-year-old.'

Oh! Well, that certainly explained a lot! I wasn't surprised as such, and I certainly wasn't ashamed to learn this. I just wondered what came next: *OK, what happens now? Do I get a badge, or what?* Thankfully, I got a *lot* more than that.

Once I was diagnosed as dyslexic, the university fixed me up with a nifty piece of computer software called Dragon. It read my course textbooks and assignments to me, and allowed me to dictate my essays into it to be printed out. This innovation was an absolute lifesaver. *Boom!* All of a sudden, I wasn't trying to run a race with both legs tied together!

That computer program changed everything for me. It enabled me to study and express myself properly and get a decent degree at the end of the course. It is still an invaluable aid for me today – believe you me, I certainly wouldn't be able to write books like *Making It*, or this one, if I didn't have Dragon!

It's weird. I was never ashamed of not being able to read, because it wasn't my fault, but I still knew there was a stigma attached to it. Too often, society looks down on people who are a bit different or who have a disability, and I guess that is partly why I kept shtum about my problem until Jade outed me.

Yet here's the crux of it. *Here's* the life lesson. If you're lucky enough to get help and encouragement to tackle a major issue in your life, I think you should try to give the same kind of assistance and hope to anybody facing the same situation. And that was why I made a TV show that told the world that I can't read.

Through my production company, Hungry Jay Media, I made a documentary for the BBC called *Jay Blades: Learning to Read at 51*. I'm not going to lie: some of my friends couldn't believe I was laying myself open like that. 'Woah, Jay, man!' they said. 'What are you doing? How did they persuade you to do *that*?'

And my reply amazed them. 'Nobody persuaded me,' I said.

'I wanted to do it. It was my idea. I suggested it.' Because the thing is, I still can't *really* read. I'm better than I was: I've learned a few tricks and shortcuts, and my Dragon software has opened a lot of doors for me. But sit down and read a book, like a non-dyslexic person? Nah. I can't do that and I have to accept, at this time in my life, I may never be able to.

I wanted to do it, but *Jay Blades: Learning to Read at 51* was an incredibly hard programme to make. If I am honest, I had no idea exactly how difficult it would be for me, emotionally. I laid myself bare because the point of the documentary was to show how demanding living with dyslexia is. And how many people do it.

I mean, just look at the figures. I learned from doing the programme that in 2022 a quarter of all kids in England didn't meet the Ofsted expected standard for reading at the end of primary school. Eight million adults in the UK have poor literacy skills. Half the people in prison can't read: that's a vicious circle, because a lot of kids who can't read end up in the nick. It seems pretty clear to me that they can't get jobs so they turn to crime.

How do you begin to get across what dyslexia is like? I did it like this: 'The only way I can explain reading is, imagine giving yourself a headache,' I said at the start of the show. 'It's pure pain.' And I wasn't exaggerating. Over the next hour, the depths of my disability became clear. Which was what I wanted.

On the show, a speech and language expert tried to teach me phonics – the basic building blocks of language, which kids normally learn at school when they're five years old. She held up simple words and asked me to make the sound of the first letter in the word. One of them was 'egg'.

'Er, egg?' I guessed. 'No, ey? Er? Hold on . . . er, eh?'

'Umbrella' was another word, with a helpful picture to explain it. This one had me proper stumped.

'Umber . . . umber . . . umber . . . um?' I suggested.

'Just the initial sound,' she explained, patiently. 'Which is u, like in up.'

'U, up, upbrella, umbrella, u . . .' I said, striving to understand. 'Wow! This is hard!'

It was tough, and raw, and I felt incredibly exposed. Once or twice, it all got too much for me. 'It's stupidly simple but insanely hard,' I sighed as I failed to master reading a simple leaflet. 'What I feel like doing now is just throwing this on the floor and just saying ***** to it all!'

I told stories as well – stories from my own life. There was the time I got a letter from a hospital. I knew it was important but there was no way I could tell what it said. So, I went out in the street and asked a passer-by to read it to me. It sounds weird to you, yeah? Well, it didn't to me. That was my normal.

It took six months to make *Jay Blades: Learning to Read at 51* and it was one of the most challenging and painful things I've ever done. Yet all the way through at the back of my mind were the many people in the same boat who might see the show and be helped by it. They were who I made it for. And I'm delighted to say it reached many of them. The reaction to the programme was unbelievable. I've never had as much feedback from anything I've done. It has been humbling to get so many messages from people who have wanted to tell me about the impact it has had on their lives.

Even now, more than a year since it aired, I still get texts, emails and messages on my socials. The thing that people say the most is, 'We don't often see someone like yourself, who has made it, talking about that thing we're ashamed of.' And they *shouldn't* be ashamed of it, but they are.

Where does that shame come from? It comes from them thinking the same thing that I used to think because I couldn't read or write: that they're stupid. They've probably been told that. They think, *I'm dumb,* but they are *not* dumb – they have a condition called dyslexia. It's a very, very different thing.

Kirsty Young interviewed me after the show came out. Her husband, Nick Jones, owns private members clubs including Soho House, but he was rubbish at school because he is dyslexic. Kirsty said the programme brought him to tears, and he sent me the following message: 'Thank you so much for making that show.'

I loved that message because it demonstrated two points. One was that having dyslexia doesn't have to hold you back: I mean, Nick Jones ain't done too bad for himself, has he? Nor has the dyslexic Richard Branson! The other point was that *Jay Blades: Learning to Read at 51* had had exactly the effect that I wanted it to.

You've always got to give back in this life. Whenever I mentor young people, I explain to them: 'If you have an influence, use it for the advantage of other people. Don't use it for yourself. Help others to move forward.' And, you know what? If you absorb that particular life lesson, you won't go too far wrong . . .

'If you have an influence, use it for the advantage of other people. Don't use it for yourself. Help others to move forward.'

3

MISTAKES

'Mistakes are perfect – as long as you learn from them'

OK, I bet this particular saying has got you doing a double-take, with a big question mark over your bonce. You probably think I've lost the plot. 'Mistakes are perfect? What you on about, Jay, you nutter? Don't you know anything? Mistakes are when you do something wrong!'

Well, hold on a minute! Hear me out! Yeah, you're right, mistakes *are* when you do something wrong, but that is only half the story. Only the start of the process. Because the import-ant bit is not when you make a mistake in your life, but what you do *next* – how you react to it. Which brings me to what I believe is a super-important life lesson: 'Mistakes are perfect – as long as you learn from them.'

You start making mistakes right from when you're a baby. Your mum trains you to use a potty and of course you get it wrong at first. But your caregiver shows you how you did it wrong, and the next time, you learn to improve your aim. *Yeah!* That wee and poo ends up in the potty!

It might sound silly, but I think you need to carry that toddler attitude through into your adult life. You look at the mistakes you've made and see them as the stepping stones into getting things right. Sometimes the mistakes are messy and sometimes they're painful. But as you get older, it's down to you to clear them up. Because your mum and dad aren't there to do it.

Nobody wants to admit to making mistakes nowadays. Everybody likes to pretend their life is idyllic. Just look at social media! From a quick glance, you'd think that everyone is always laughing, drinking, dancing, holidaying in Dubai, living their best life. You'd think the world is perfect . . . except that it really, really isn't.

'Mistakes are perfect – as long as you learn from them.'

Nobody wants to show their mistakes. It's as though people believe that a mistake will do to you what Kryptonite does to Superman – it will destroy you! Yet speaking from my own experience, all of my mistakes have helped me. They have helped me to learn lessons and to develop as a person.

Michael Jordan has a great saying. He says, 'I have missed so many shots, yet the only ones that people talk about are the ones that won the game.' Well, he is the greatest basketball player ever because he saw what he was doing wrong on the shots that he missed and used that knowledge to move forward. He *learned*.

We all make mistakes but, to use another sporting analogy, I see those mistakes as like my starting blocks on an athletics track. Any setback is a disappointment, but not if you use it as a starting block to catapult you in the direction that you need to go. And then you can set off again like Usain Bolt!

After you've made a bad mistake, or had a setback, it's only human nature to feel down for a while. I'm no different. I might spend a day or two stewing and feeling sorry for myself: thinking, *oh, Jay, you screwed up there!* But it's never any longer than that, and then – *Bosh!* I'm ready to rock and roll again!

I've always been resilient in that way. I'm glad that I am. I'm not entirely sure where it comes from but I think it's rooted in that naivety that I keep going on about. There's something in my nature that just makes me think, *everything is going to be all right. I've made a mistake, but it's all going to be OK*.

It's lucky that I have that quality, that bouncebackability, because as I said at the start of this book, I've made plenty of mistakes in my life! I've made mistakes in relationships, in jobs and in my attitudes. I sometimes think I'm the sort of geezer who just walks off the edges of cliffs by mistake. Yet, somehow, I'm still here.

And there's a lesson to take from that. Anybody who makes major mistakes and who comes out the other end needs to think, *right, there's a reason why that happened.* And when you've made enough mistakes, and learned from them all, that's when you understand who you are, and you find your path through life.

Phew! Heavy stuff, right? But I really believe it's true. We can all learn from our mistakes right from childhood, and it's mega-important that we do. Because if we don't take note of

'Every father should remember that, one day, his children will follow his example and not his advice.'

the important lessons, we can end up being the kind of parents who damage our *own* children's childhoods.

Here's another thought I put on my social media one time: 'Every father should remember that, one day, his children will follow his example and not his advice.' Not that it ever applied to me: I never got an example *or* any advice from The Man Who Contributed Towards My Birth, because he was never there! This meant that I never had a father figure, a male role model, in my life to learn from. So, when I was younger, I made mistake after mistake after mistake – especially in relationships, and how I behaved around women – and it's very easy to blame all of that on my absent father. Very easy. *Too* easy.

Because, you know what? I can't put everything that I did wrong down to me not having a dad. I think that would just be a cop-out and a convenient excuse. I was angry with him but, as I've got older, I don't blame TMWCTMB for anything, because I've realized I don't know his full story. I mean, sure, having more than twenty kids and abandoning a lot of them seems bang out of order, to say the least. But he must have had issues that warranted him behaving the way he did. We are all shaped by our experiences in our early years and, when it comes down to it, I don't have a Scooby what his were like.

How was he treated when he was a boy in Jamaica? How did it affect him when his parents emigrated to London and only sent for him later? What was his life like when he moved over here and started sowing his seed in the sixties? I don't know, so how can I reach a condemnatory judgement on him?

Even in my fifties, I still don't really understand why The Man Who Contributed Towards My Birth absented himself from my life. But who am I to say to him, 'Oh, you should have acted like *this*?' And I don't like going down that road anyway. I don't like pointing the finger at other people. I prefer to point it at myself.

OK, let's say that TMWCTMB *has* made major mistakes in his life. Well, I can take lessons from them, even if he can't. I can learn not to do the same things that he did (or, rather, that he *didn't* do) because otherwise I might repeat his sins and continue his legacy of neglect. And I want to break that cycle.

One big mistake I made in my life through not having a father figure, a male role model to turn to for help, was getting involved in extreme violence. I met a lot of racism as a kid growing up in Hackney, mainly at secondary school, and, as I said in *Making It*, I decided early doors the only way to fight it was with my fists.

There were a lot of nasty, racist words being thrown around in playgrounds and on the streets in the eighties and I adopted a zero-tolerance attitude towards them. If a kid pushed me, or called me a 'wog' or a 'coon', they were getting a smack in the mouth right away. That attitude got me into a lot of fights and a lot of grief.

Now that I am a lot older and wiser, of course, I know that violence is never the answer to anything, but it was a big part of my early life. And, sure, it's very hard to argue with anyone who says that getting involved in fights and aggro is a big mistake – but, at the same time, I can understand exactly why I did it.

Basically, there was a lot of racist violence aimed at little kids by bigger boys in my secondary school, and the teachers just didn't want to know. If you said what was going on, they just didn't listen, and told you to shut up. And, if *they* weren't going to protect us, what was left but for us to do it ourselves?

I was a confident lad and not afraid to stand up to the bullies but some other kids weren't so lucky. There were one or two lovely, but shy and timid, boys in my year who used to get a right beating at breaktimes, and I made it my mission not just to stand up for myself but to try to defend them as well. Does that qualify as a mistake, or is there such a thing as *good violence*? Ha! Even with my philosophy degree, I'm not sure I'm equipped to answer *that* one, but I can still recognize why I behaved like that back then – and when I've told a lot of people about my early days, it's got a very interesting reaction from them.

When *Making It* was published, I gave a few talks and did Q&A sessions in bookshops. I did one event where I was asked about my hot-headed fighting years and I explained that I had made it my business to sort out any bullies or racists who bothered me – and after I said it, everybody in the room started clapping.

Wow! I've got to say, that was quite a headfuck to have 500 people – and they were smart, book-reading people – applauding me for being violent! These were the kind of people who'd normally condemn all violence out-of-hand. But when I explained the context of what I'd been through, it seemed admirable to them.

Weird, eh? But I think I know why it happened. I reckon a lot of people have been bullied at some point in their lives, and maybe nobody ever stood up for them. So, when they hear stories and experiences like mine, it resonates with them. They like what I did even if, deep down, they know that they shouldn't!

Like I say, though, mistakes are only perfect because you can learn from them. It took me a while to realize that I couldn't just go around thumping the people that I didn't agree with or I didn't like – and the penny only really dropped when I went to Oxford, at twenty-one, to do my volunteer work at Cyrenians.

Working in the Cyrenians homeless hostel grounded me in a way that nothing else up until that point ever had. Being with people who were even less fortunate than me gave me a different perspective. It was like moving from your childhood home, where you'd always lived a certain way, to another house with new people, and realizing, *Oh, there are different ground rules here!*

I met these geezers who had nothing in the world, and I realized that in a lot of the cases, it was violence – often, violence resulting from alcohol abuse – that had brought them down to where they were. It was an epiphany for me, a wake-up call, and it curbed my violent behaviour. I just put a complete stop to it.

It was a lesson well learned, and one that I'm still applying thirty years on. I'm happy to say that I get a lot fewer insults chucked my way nowadays, but racism hasn't just gone away. However, if anyone makes a racist comment to me now, I'm not about to smack them one.

It hardly ever happens face-to-face, anyway. When I get racially abused nowadays, it's nearly always on social media. Some, ahem, *brave*, keyboard warrior will rear up and chuck a few nasty words my way. And, do you know what I do? I ignore them. I just think, *whatever, mate,* and I move on with my day.

Because it's not worth doing anything else. I don't engage with the racists or the haters because their negativity is not my problem. I don't need it in my rucksack. They throw their comments out because they want attention, they want me to bite and fight back . . . and I don't want to give them that satisfaction. There's only one key I need to press: *BLOCK*.

You know what I mean? I don't know what's happened to those people in their lives to make them how they are, and they don't know *me*, even if they think they do because they see me on the telly. And I suggest you do the same thing if trolls ever start bugging you: *BLOCK! BLOCK! BLOCK!* Because life is too short.

Coming back to this chapter's theme of 'mistakes are perfect', I freely admit that most people would struggle to see it as 'perfect' to get nicked for possession of drugs and end up with a police record, like I did back in the day. But it was good for me, because it taught me yet another valuable life lesson. Coming from where I did, there was not a lot in the way of opportunity. So, when someone says, 'Do you want to earn some easy money?', it is very tempting.

Young people in inner-city areas are striving for economic independence. When you are trying to become a man, you don't want to keep running to your mum for pocket money. You want to make your own money, and if somebody comes along and offers you a naughty way of doing it – *Bang!* You want some of that! Growing up, I'd see these big men around me who didn't have jobs but who had money and cars and respect, and I'd be, like, *Wow! That's the way to do it!*

There will always be judgemental people who say, 'Oh, you

shouldn't do petty crime' but *shouldn't* is a big word, isn't it? There *shouldn't* be poverty. There *shouldn't* be food banks. What are the people who are striving to survive meant to do? You do all sorts of wrong shit when you're desperate.

The social commentators proclaiming that drug dealing and such-like is wrong are normally in pretty comfortable circumstances. They are doing OK for themselves. These 'experts' need to reflect that not everybody is lucky enough to have their nice lives and give more thought and sympathy to those who are struggling.

Having said all that, dealing drugs, even at the most lowly level, is never going to end well. You know what you are doing is criminal, you know the police are out to get you, and you know the danger of getting nicked. You accept that risk: it's just how things are. It's the rules of the game.

So, when the Old Bill booted my door in early one morning and I got hauled off to court and charged with possession, part of me thought, *Fair enough. It's all in the game.* I got a £50 fine and a criminal record, and I knocked it on the head. I'm glad I did, because some people I know ended up in way, way more grief than that.

You learn from your mistakes but, if I can get deep here just for a minute, I think that sometimes the worst mistakes you make, the ones that you really *don't* want to make, are inevitable. You're in the matrix: bad stuff is going to happen whatever you do, and all you can do is gain the life wisdom to turn it around.

People say the apple doesn't fall far from the tree, and we are all destined to repeat the sins of our fathers. I'm not sure about that, but I know one thing: when I was young and working out who I was, the one big mistake that I was *desperate* not to make was to scatter kids around by different women, like my dad had.

It's well known now that TMWCTMB fathered a lot of kids – twenty-seven, at the last count – and didn't have much to do with a lot of them, me included. I have to admit, this filled me with incredulity and disgust for the longest time: *How the hell can he do it? How can he not care about us children he has created?*

I had such contempt for how my dad had lived – and yet I have found myself with three children, by three different women, none of whom I now live with. That's what life can do to you. You have all these plans and resolutions, and then you find that life has written its own script for you and you have no choice but to follow it.

I was hardly out of my teens when I had my first son, Levi. I was super-young but when my on–off girlfriend, Maria, said she was pregnant, I was delighted. For one thing, I was happy that I had some lead in my pencil! But, seriously, most of all I just thought, *Yay! I'm going to be a dad! I'm going to be a man!*

When he was born, I thought Levi was the best thing since sliced bread, but when I tried to knuckle down to being a dad, it didn't come easy to me. It didn't feel natural. I fed the little guy and burped him, and changed his nappies, but I felt . . . trapped. Maria and I weren't getting on and, after a year, I split.

I know that doesn't look good written down on paper and I'm not proud of it – but I'm not exactly *ashamed* of it, either. It's just life. The hard truth is that I was too young and immature to be a dad, emotionally and mentally. It took me a long time to see that. Thirty years on, it's incredibly clear to me.

My second lad, Dior, came along four years later. He wasn't born into the most promising of circumstances. Me and his mum, Lisa, had split up but would still get together occasionally for the odd night. I never thought to check that she was still taking contraception and it was a total shock when I learned she was pregnant.

After I got the news, Lisa and I tried to make a go of it again and we moved back in together before Dior was born. But she and I had run our course, we were arguing like mad, and the atmosphere in the house was so tense and toxic that, after a few months, Lisa moved out, taking Dior with her.

It sounds like a litany of personal failures, right? Well, there is certainly no bigger mistake that a man can make than to father a child and then not stick around. In a way, I hold my hands up but, in my defence, there is a big, big difference between me and TMWCTMB – and that difference is that I have always been a big part of my kids' lives.

You don't *regret* having a kid. I loved all three of my children from the day they were born and, even though I wasn't *ready* to have the first two when I did, I knew I wanted to be – I *had* to be – in their lives. It was simple. Because having no dad would not be good for them. Like it hadn't been good for me.

One of the most important life lessons of all is that life is never black and white. Traditionalists say parents should always stay together for the kids – but if mum and dad are at war, how healthy is *that* environment for the child to grow up in? In the real world, every situation is different. There's no one-size-fits-all right and wrong.

I'm guessing the people who are quickest to condemn failed relationships and broken families come from very settled backgrounds. Their parents may have been together for fifty years, and maybe their grandparents were the same before that. That stability is their norm and what they know.

Well, it's not an excuse and it's not meant to be one, but I never had that. If I can use an analogy: imagine growing up in Africa, where you've never seen snow. Then you move to England on a winter's day: it is going to shock you! Everything will seem alien. And that's what settled family life felt like to me.

The people who are quick to criticize have to understand the environment that some others grow up in is not the same as theirs. When you've never experienced nuclear family life as a child, you don't understand it, and if you don't understand it, how can you *be* it? Especially if you have a kid when you're still dead young.

Mind you, I wasn't young when I split from my ex-wife, Jade, and moved out from living with her and our daughter, Zola.

I was in my mid-forties. We had a long and loving marriage until the love died a little – and when our marriage ended, it killed me. In fact, as I explained in *Making It*, it hit me so hard that I actually wanted to kill myself.

We're talking about mistakes right now – well, as I drove away from my family home, and my beloved eight-year-old daughter, I felt like my entire *life* had been one big mistake. I felt a complete failure: useless and pathetic. It took me a long time, and I needed the help of very special people, to come through that one.

Yet I'm not after sympathy here. This is a book of life lessons, not self-pity! I've had my hard times, but I'm sure you have, too. I'm not unique in going through painful break-ups and making repeated mistakes. For me, the whole point is how you get through them and improve. How you *learn* from them.

As I say, whatever I have been through, and no matter how hard it's got, I have always been in my children's lives. For a long time, I didn't have much money but I did what I could for them. Nowadays, I'm lucky enough to be able to help them out more financially. But I've always been *there* for them.

Without getting sickly, I love my three kids more than anything else in the world. They're all independent spirits, and I like that about them, but they all know they can call me any time they want to. Having grown up without a dad to give me that support, I've made damn sure they haven't gone through the same.

And you know what? My kids will make mistakes as well. Maybe not the same ones as I have, but they'll make mistakes all through their lives. And I hope, if and when they ask me, I'll be able to help them turn them into *perfect* mistakes by learning from them and improving themselves. Which is the point of it all.

Because we all make mistakes, in our families and in general life, and we can all learn from them. We can move on. Tomorrow is always a new day. In fact, here's another of my favourite sayings for you: 'Regardless of how filthy your past has been, your future is still spotless.'

Think about it! Whatever bad stuff you may have done in the past, it's still in your power to give yourself a blinding future. Tomorrow is always a new day. If you're willing to learn, and have the right attitude, you can take a blank piece of paper and write yourself a new reality. If I can do it, anyone can!

'Regardless of how filthy your past has been, your future is still spotless.'

You can do it – as long as people give you a chance. Sadly not everyone is always willing to do this. Take prisoners: they come out of jail, and the principle is that they have served their time and been rehabilitated and are ready to take their place as useful members of society again. Except that some people won't let them. There are always those who will look at them and say, 'Well, yeah, you've served your time, but you're still a robber!

A lowlife! You don't deserve a second chance!' And what are they supposed to do, if people just write them off like that?

If this sounds like your life, I would say that, ideally, you need to move to a new environment. If that's not practical, get a different set of people around you who can help to give you a better mindset. Or develop that mindset yourself. Because you can't live your true life if you're being defined and limited by other people's opinions.

Sometimes, if I'm working with or mentoring young people, I will tell them, 'No one wins at chess by only moving forwards.' Which is true: nobody ever became a grandmaster by charging down the board at a million miles an hour, right? They'd be losing knights and pawns left, right and centre!

No, sometimes you need to go backwards to go forwards. There may be a few lucky, golden people for whom everything falls into place, but most of us slowly try to make our way forwards every day. Something happens that sets us back, and we fall down. But then we get up, dust ourselves down and move on.

We have to have those setbacks, those knocks and bruises, in life to appreciate the good times. It's like going to the gym. You can't just turn up, sign in, then turn around and go home with the body you've always dreamed of! No, you have to

'No one wins at chess by only moving forwards.'

work out, and you have to work hard. You're there in the gym and you don't see any results at first, but then you feel a bit fitter and stronger. You might get an injury and it sets you back, maybe even right back to square one, but then you go again. You'll feel you've gone backwards, but you get the forward motion going again. And it's worth it. *Always* worth it.

So, what's the moral of this tale then, Jay? Simple! There's no such thing as the perfect life. We might imagine that celebrities are leading the perfect life – and then suddenly we hear they're getting divorced and footage comes out showing them arguing and fighting, or worse. And you think, *Wow! Even* their *lives are not perfect!*

So, don't believe the movies, or the TV shows, or the social media posts of people claiming they are always living their best life and sipping champagne in Ibiza! Because it's a fiction. The only perfect life that exists is one that includes perfect mistakes. And only *then* if we use them to make us better . . .

4

SELF-RESPECT

'The way you treat yourself sets the standard for others'

Now, here we go – this particular topic is one that I feel very strongly about. I suppose, in some ways, it's obvious, and yet it's easy to lose sight of it. I can't say it enough times: we all want other people to respect us, yet if we don't respect *ourselves*, it's just not going to happen.

How do you respect yourself? For one thing, you don't let yourself get treated like a doormat. I've learned that, sadly, there are lots of people out there who like to treat others in that way. There are always those who like to take advantage and, if you let them walk all over you, they will do exactly that.

You know the type. You might have friends like it, or even family. You never hear a dicky bird from them when things are going well for them, then they suddenly ring up when they want something: 'Can you do this for me?' 'Yeah, OK!' you say. Because, after all, they're friends or family!

It goes quiet again for a couple of months – they never ring just to check in, or to see how you're doing – and then they're on the blower again: 'Right, can you get me *this*?' And you might start wondering: *Hmm. It seems to me like you only get in touch when you want something. And I don't like getting played, mate!*

I'm afraid it's just a fact of life: if you are always there for those people whenever they need you, you *will* get used and abused. It's going to happen. And personally, I'd prefer to deal with people who are doing things for others, rather than just for themselves. That way, you spread a bit more love around.

'Mental strength is incredibly important, so take care of your mind and the way you speak to yourself.'

I'm not saying you need to dump users, or be horrible to them. There's no need for that. But you sometimes have to be a little selfish to protect yourself. We all know how to keep in shape physically: there's tons of advice out there about that. But improving your *mental* strength is just as important, and can be a lot trickier. Without it, you have nothing. I posted something on my socials a while back which I think is very true: 'Mental strength is incredibly important, so take care of your mind and the way you speak to yourself.'

The good thing is that society is changing, and nowadays people aren't afraid to talk about their mental health. It wasn't always like that! Back when I was a kid, in the seventies and eighties, there was a proper stigma attached to mental health. You'd never say you felt a bit down because everyone would just take the piss and laugh at you. You had to tough it out and pretend you were on top of your game.

There were no allowances made at all for people who were going through a hard time in their head, where nobody could see it. Twenty years ago, the boxer Frank Bruno got sectioned to be treated for depression and bipolar disorder, and the front page of *The Sun* newspaper said:

BONKERS BRUNO LOCKED UP

I mean, *can you Adam-and-Eve it?* It was just so cruel, and heartless, and uncaring about what the poor guy was going through. We have come a long way since those dark days, thankfully, but mental strength is still incredibly precious, and we have to do all that we can to treat ourselves well and maintain it.

It will probably surprise you if you've seen me on *The Repair Shop*, being all jovial and hail-fellow-well-met with everyone around me, but I am actually an extreme introvert. I *know* that I am, because I did a proper personality test when I went on a business course, and that was the result that came out!

It's called the Myers-Briggs Type Indicator® assessment and it's basically a questionnaire about your likes, your dislikes and other aspects of your personality. When the people running the course told me that I registered as an extreme introvert, you could have knocked me down with a feather. But then, when I thought harder about it, it made a lot more sense.

I'm on TV and I'm high-profile nowadays but, given the choice, I'd always prefer to be at home, in a room on my own, listening to music. It's just the way I am. I need time on my own, to reflect and to repair, and to get back in touch with myself and look after myself. If I'm honest, I've been an introvert ever since I was a kid.

Believe it or not, when I was a lad, I was ultra-shy. If I was around adults, I would hardly say a word. Some of the elders used to see that, get me wrong and say that I was sly, but it wasn't that. I was just being a sponge, taking in everything that was going on around me. Without knowing it, I was protecting myself.

Taking care of myself in that way was good for my mental strength and it's a good thing that I did it, because school certainly didn't build up my self-respect! In fact, they told me I was useless. 'It's not even worth talking to you, Blades,' the careers teacher told me, when I left. '*You'll* never amount to anything.'

That sort of stuff can do a lot of damage to a kid's sense of self-worth, but luckily, in my case, I never believed it! Even though I'm an introvert, I still had a ridiculous amount of self-confidence and I always believed I'd do well when I found my way in life. God knows where that belief comes from! But

I'm glad that I have it. I'm very aware, though, that not every-body is lucky enough to have my mad level of confidence. When a young person is told by their elders that they are useless, a lot of them believe it because they know no better. They don't treat themselves well and they kind of give up . . . which can lead them to drink and drugs.

I dabbled with both of them, like any teenager, but they weren't for me. I didn't like how they made me feel out of control and messy. I needed all my wits about me in Hackney in those days and being strung-out and vulnerable wasn't an option.

The other reason I didn't get big into drink or drugs was that I could see how they had messed up a lot of people that I knew. You're not treating yourself well if you're getting into a state where you look terrible and you don't even know what you're doing, and I could see plenty of examples around me in Hackney.

I'd clock some geezer not much older than me, stumbling along looking like a right tramp. 'Hold up!' I'd say to a friend. 'Didn't he use to be a well cool, smart guy? *Woah!* What happened to him?' And the answer was always drink, or weed, or coke, or worse. I'd see the mess it had made of them and think, *No, thanks!*

It didn't only happen to geezers. I would see women who had been beautiful, real around-the-way girls that all the boys wanted to get with, and I'd hardly even recognize them: 'Shit – what happened to *her*?' And it would be the same answer.

Booze. Hash. And then they'd get treated badly because they had no self-respect.

'Stop thinking too much! It's all right not to know all the answers.' Your mind can play all kinds of tricks with you. Some people worry themselves crazy all the time. My wife, Lisa, is a bit like that. She will worry herself nuts over stuff we have no control over. If we're going out, Lisa will say, 'What shall we do if the weather turns nasty?' or 'What if we get into an accident in the car?'

Well, I've got an answer to that, and it's one I put up on social media a few weeks ago: 'Stop thinking too much! It's all right not to know all the answers.' Because if you think too hard about what might happen in the future, or what could go wrong, it over-complicates everything. You end up tying yourself in mental knots.

I'll say to Lisa, 'OK, let's imagine that *does* happen and we crash the car, what will we do?'

'I don't know,' she might say.

'Well, we'll check everyone is OK, then we'll sort it all out.'

'But what if . . . ?' she will say.

'Well, then we'll . . .'

We talk it out and talk it out and eventually Lisa will smile and say, 'All of that isn't going to happen, is it?' By then, we could already have done the journey and got safely home! I don't mind: I'm lucky I've never got anxious in that way, but some people are born worriers, and you try to help them. Especially if you love them.

That's definitely a major life lesson, for me: don't think too hard. You can never know all the answers. Nobody does! Even Professor Stephen Hawking must have had stuff that stumped him! So, I never over-think what might happen, or over-prepare for things. I'd rather jump right in and see what happens. If you don't think too hard, you can't get too anxious!

That's how I work on *The Repair Shop*. If we're going to film a scene, I don't want to be there an hour before. I don't even want to be there ten minutes before! I'd rather get there bang on time and go straight into it – *bosh! Let's do this!*

When a guest is bringing an object into the workshop for repair, I don't want to know anything in advance except for that person's name. There are so many emails going around before they arrive: where they're from, what the object is, how old it is, what's wrong with it, etc, etc, etc. I never read a single one of them.

I don't *want* to know all that information because it would clutter my mind up. It would get in the way. I want to hear that person's story, and all about their item, for the first time when I meet them, because then the conversation will flow and my surprise will be totally natural. It's my favourite part of the show!

Don't overthink things. Just go with the flow: with the human interaction. I know if I was super-briefed about a guest and their story, and trying to steer the chat in a direction the producers wanted, I'd mess up and fluff it. It would not go well. So, I just try to keep my mind free and open – the same as I do in everyday life.

Of course, there is a big irony here. Here am I, holding forth about mental health and the best ways to build your mental strength, and dishing out life lessons on how to treat yourself and respect yourself – and I haven't always followed them. Because some years ago, I had a nervous breakdown.

I think my story is quite well known now but I'll tell it anyway, just in case you have been lucky enough to avoid hearing it before! Back in 2015, I was still living in High Wycombe with my ex-wife, Jade, and our daughter, Zola, but our marriage was going wrong.

The atmosphere between Jade and me was pretty grim. She and I had been running two charity ventures between us, Street Dreams and Out of the Dark, and the end of our relationship brought them crashing down as well, which hurt a lot of people. In the middle of it all, I was just about holding myself together, and then, suddenly . . . I wasn't.

One evening, I snapped. *I broke.* I told Jade 'I'm going!' and I walked out of our house without a bag or even taking my phone. I got in my car and, with no idea where or *why* I was going, I just drove, for hours and hours and hours, along a motorway and into a deep, dark night. I wasn't thinking. I wasn't *anything*.

It was a proper, full-on breakdown. I wanted to drive my car into a motorway bridge and end it all, and only the protective metal barriers around them stopped me doing it. I drove and drove and drove until I just couldn't drive any more and then I pulled off the motorway, found a car park and parked.

Where the hell am I? As it happened, I was in Wolverhampton, but I didn't know and I didn't care. I sat in my car for days, not even knowing who I was any more. I felt as if everything I had ever done, I had ever been, had been worthless and pointless. And I felt that *I* was worthless and pointless.

It was weird because, to an outsider, my life at that point probably looked pretty pukka. I had everything most people would want. I was in a long-term relationship, and raising a great kid, in a lovely house. I was co-running two cool charities that I loved and that gave me a lot of joy. So, how did I get so *broken*?

Well, looking back, I know exactly how, and that knowledge leads to probably the most important life lesson in this entire book. Sitting in that car park for days on end, I felt I had failed at my relationship; failed at business; failed at *life*. But I was missing the fundamental point that led to my collapse:

I had failed at communicating.

I mean, big time! I had stopped telling people how I was feeling. I had a lot of stuff on my plate and I was trying to handle it all without any help, or telling anybody that I was struggling. I kept everything bottled up and I forgot the most important, crucial tip for mental strength: *never* stop communicating.

I was putting myself under a lot of pressure in those days. It wasn't just falling out of love with Jade and it wasn't just work stresses. In addition to that, I was totally enmeshed in the local community back then, and it was taking a heavy toll on me. It was damaging me without me realizing it.

Somehow, I'd become the geezer that everyone turned to for help. I seemed to be an unofficial, unpaid community-support officer. Seriously: it got to the point where I felt that I could hardly leave the house without being stopped and asked for advice . . . and some of the problems were proper, proper heavy.

Working with troubled kids via our charities, I knew a lot of High Wycombe's more challenged families. One mother had a son who had moved out and was always in bother with the law. She came to me in a state because he'd been in court again and the judge had said he'd spare him jail . . . but only if he moved back to live with his mum.

His mother loved him but he was a nightmare to live with because he'd steal stuff from her and bring all sorts of trouble to the house. She was also worried that he was influencing his younger brother, who was beginning to go off the rails. 'I'm worried sick, 24/7!' she told me. 'What should I do, Jay?'

How do you answer that? I just gave her my honest reaction. 'It's not fair on you,' I said. 'I think you have to say no and send him to prison.' Which, obviously, had her distraught and bawling her eyes out.

I had people coming up to me telling me they were victims of domestic violence and asking me to find them a way out. There were girls saying that they were being sexually abused. It felt like I was dealing with issues non-stop, every time I popped out for a pint of milk. It was exhausting!

In a way, I felt proud that people came to me with their problems like that, but, combined with the hard times I was having in my own life, it was all dragging me down. *Very* down. And the worst thing was that when it came to my time to need help, I felt I had no one to turn to.

In my muddled head, it would have been too much of a role reversal. I had tried to help and protect all these troubled people for years – how could I turn round now and start weighing them down with *my* bother? Who could *I* communicate with? I felt like the answer was nobody, and so I just stayed quiet and I stewed.

I shut down. And that is the thing that you should *never* do.

It was never going to end well and it didn't. It ended with my breakdown and days of sitting, lost and empty, in a car park. Yet some guardian angels in human form came to my rescue, and helped me to build a new life, and you know what? I think now that my breakdown was the best thing that ever happened to me!

I know it sounds crazy, but I mean it. It felt like the end of the world, *my* world, but it got me out of the dark place I was in. It helped me to realize who I am and what I want. It was another of those *perfect mistakes* because without it, there is no way that I would be where I am today.

I look at my life nowadays and – touch wood – it's not too shabby. I'm doing TV work that I love. I've got my own production company. I recently got married again and, the most important thing of all, I am happy. Thank God I never drove into that bridge!

Going back to this chapter's theme, I had stopped treating myself well and I had stopped *looking after myself* and I paid the price. A very big, scary price. But as I keep saying, mistakes are there to be learned from, and the main thing for me is to take better care of myself and ensure that it never happens again.

I can't say one hundred per cent that it never will. Mental strength is a very fragile thing. You can't guarantee anything in this life. But I recognize the warning signs that led to my breakdown now, and I'd like to think that if they ever raise their ugly heads again, I'll know what to do.

What are the warning signs? All of the things I've just been talking about. If I started *going into myself* again. If I was closing down. If I was worrying, and over-thinking, and over-analysing everything. And, worst of all, if I was keeping it all to myself . . . but now, I wouldn't do that.

The big mistake I made when I really started to struggle was not talking to anyone. Nobody knew what was going on. Now, if there is another time, I'll know to talk to the people around me, the people I love, and say, 'Everything's getting on top of me. It's all too much. I need help.'

I've realized that I need to treat myself well and value my mental health. Part of that is accepting what that Myers-Briggs test told me: I'm an extreme introvert. The geezer that everyone sees on TV isn't necessarily what's inside of me. I have to make time for myself to unwind and take the pressure off.

I've had to learn to say 'No' to stuff. I always help people when I can, but I have to admit there are times it all gets well overwhelming. I sometimes have a look at my socials, or log in to my LinkedIn, and the sheer number of people asking me for stuff does my head in:

'Jay, can you get me into TV?'

'Will you help me be on *The Repair Shop*?'

'Can I come and work for you?'

'When can we arrange a Zoom to fix up you appearing on my podcast?'

'Jay, my dad in Scotland loves your show but he's got Alzheimer's – will you come and visit him?'

Most people are nice enough, but some get proper demanding, and there just aren't enough hours in the day to do it all. Not when I'm filming five days a week and have a million other things going on. It's the lesson I've learned: I can't take too much on, or I just collapse under the weight of it all.

I've learned how to treat myself and to set the standard for how others treat me. When I'm filming *The Repair Shop*, it's full-on all day: meeting the guests, talking to producers, talking to the crew. It's non-stop, and I know it could easily wear me down if I let it. So, I don't let it.

'You have the answer. You just have to keep quiet enough to hear it.'

Each morning, I have breakfast in a corner on my own. All the experts and crew know to leave me alone: '*Don't bother Jay, he's just doing his thing!*' They all know it's nothing personal. It's just me taking a deep breath and setting myself up for the day. For what's ahead. *Looking after myself.*

By the same token, I never socialize in the evenings nowadays when filming's done. I just go straight to my room, take my boots off and sit on the bed to wind down. Half the time, I wake up at three in the morning, lying on the bed still fully clothed! Well, if it works, it works. And I've found it works for me.

Here's another saying that comes to mind: 'You have the answer. You just have to keep quiet enough to hear it.' There's the key. *Learn to listen to yourself*: to your body *and* your mind. They will tell you what you need. All you need to do is pay attention.

If you ask me, a lot of people are good at following what their brains and their eyes tell them but not as smart at listening to their stomachs: their gut instinct. Your gut instinct is your first brain: your most instinctive reaction. And if it is telling you, *Oh, this doesn't feel good*, it's almost certainly right!

If anybody reading this is in a bad place mentally, like I was in 2015, here's the big thing you have to do: talk to people. Talk to family members. Talk to friends. Talk to professionals. Tell them how you feel. Don't do what I did and hide away in a corner. Open up. *Communicate.*

There are more than seven billion people in this world. Seven billion! There's got to be someone out there who will talk to you, listen hard, put an arm around your shoulders and go with you on that path to get better. If someone isn't helping you with that like they should, find somebody else who will.

By the same token, if someone comes to you saying they're not doing well, *listen* to them. Properly. Don't just say, 'Oh, you'll be fine!' and leave them be. That's *the* worst thing you can do. Listen, and ask the crucial questions:

'How do you feel?'

'What's worrying you?'

'What do you need?'

'How can I help?'

Really, just *be there for them*. Give them the human touch; we all need it, even – or especially – when we pretend that we don't. Treat them well and treat them kindly, and . . . who knows? With a bit of luck, you'll have set them back on the road to behaving the same way towards themselves.

5

COMMUNITY

*'The nice thing about teamwork is that
you always have others on your side'*

When you first start out in life, as a cocky young sod, you sometimes think that you have all of the answers. I certainly did, and a lot of good it did me! But as you grow older, and learn a few life lessons, the penny drops that you get a whole lot more done, and achieve a load more, when you're part of a team.

Actually, I have another word for teamwork. I call it 'community' because that is what it is. When I was a kid, I always knew there were people in our community, on our estate, that you could definitely rely on. They'd always have your back, and knowing that would help you to move forward.

Let me break it down into the simplest terms. Imagine you are trying to move a sofa, right? Doing it on your own is a backbreaking nightmare! You have to move one corner, then another corner, then another corner. But get a team of four of you together, and *bosh!* Suddenly, the job's a doddle!

Anything you're trying to achieve in life is easier done with community, or with teamwork. It might be a job, a marriage, a family unit, a major project. Because no matter how hard you might try, it's difficult – no; it's *impossible* – to do it all and move forward on your own. We all need help and support.

The blinding thing is that it's really easy to find a team to join. Just look out for people who share your interests. If you're into doing community work, you can volunteer and be in a team straight away. Or it might be playing football, or helping out at your local parkrun, or knitting! Just find some like-minded spirits and crack on.

If we're talking about work, teamwork is totally crucial. Looking back at my life so far, I've been lucky enough to be part of some killer teams over the years. And that has taught me that when you're starting out, and finding your way, having people in your corner can be an absolute godsend.

My first proper job, in my teens, was as a gofer and office boy in a model agency in London. It wasn't too shabby – I ask you, what teenage boy *wouldn't* like being around beautiful models? And even though I didn't know my arse from my elbow when I started, some key people there made me feel right at home. The lady who ran the gaff took a shine to me, even when I was a bit clueless, and a staff photographer named Jan took me under his wing. He showed me how to take good shots, and how dark rooms worked, and even gave me an old camera he didn't need. They supported me and it felt really, really nice.

That was like a training slope for teamwork for me, but I really learned a lot more about how important it is to have people working as a unit when I moved to the Cyrenians homeless hostel in Oxford. It was crucial there that we got things right every day because those poor residents totally depended on us. We were all they had.

I was only a volunteer there for the first few months but that didn't make me feel a lesser member of the team. The full-time staff accepted me and gave me the same duties they were doing: washing, feeding and caring for our guests. I took to it well, which was why they made me a paid staff member pretty sharpish.

The big lesson I got from that hostel, which you can apply to *any* walk of life, is how important trust is in a team. Basically, you have to know you can trust your colleagues and rely on them to do their jobs properly. It means you can get on with what you have to do without worrying about them.

In a job, in a marriage or in life in general, that trust is vital, and if it's not there, everything can – pardon my language – turn to shit. Teams work best if people are in them for the long term and work their way from the bottom to the top. It means when they take their place at the head of the table, they know how every job works.

Sadly, that didn't happen at Cyrenians. They brought in total outsiders to run the place, who didn't understand how it functioned and had a totally different vision to those of us who'd worked there for years. All the trust and team spirit that had existed was worn away and destroyed. That was why I left a job that I'd loved.

Not every job is as fulfilling as helping homeless people. After I left Cyrenians, I ended up doing building site and labouring work again for a few years. But even in straightforward roles like that, teamwork is crucial if you're going to get anything done.

It's simple work but you all depend on each other. If a labourer doesn't mix up the concrete, no one can build anything. If nobody does the groundwork, even if it's just clearing a path, how is anything going to get constructed? You all rely on one another, like we do in every walk of life.

Labouring crews might be basic teams, but you know what? They build houses! Look around you, at any house: teamwork built that! Or raise your sights higher: to amazing buildings like St Paul's Cathedral or Westminster Abbey. Do you really think that some geezer could build them on his tod?

I think some poet once said that no man is an island. Spot on! Teamwork, and community, are everything, and they are what keep people and society going. And you see them at their very best when everybody is pulling together to benefit people who need a bit of help and a leg-up. I love it when that happens.

When I met my first wife, Jade, we clicked straight away even though we were very different characters from completely contrasting backgrounds. Or maybe we clicked *because* we were very different characters from completely contrasting backgrounds. Don't they say 'opposites attract'?

I was the council-house kid from the East End streets and Jade came from a very educated family in Turkey. Yet we both shared an intensity, a drive and a wish to make the world a better place, any way we could. We had complementary attributes and it turned us into a dream team.

Together, we started our charity, Street Dreams, to help under-privileged kids, and we found that our talents dovetailed together like the perfect wood-joint. Jade was a genius at planning and admin and persuading people in power to give us a break. She opened doors I'd never have been even able to find!

Jade brought that to Street Dreams, and I brought being able to get the best out of damaged kids who needed a break. I was always able to relate to, and work with, troubled teenagers who were at war with the world, but I ask you – why *wouldn't* I be? I used to be one myself!

Jade and I turned into a brilliant team for years and we helped the hard-done-by kids we mentored to grow into team players themselves. We tried to show them that, as the old saying goes, there is no 'I' in team. They could all achieve so much more if they pulled together.

We went into local communities full of tensions, where Black, White and Asian teenagers were kicking the shit out of each other and showed them they were all in the same boat. That there was no need for them to be at war, and they would be a lot happier if they joined up to be on the same side.

Jade and I wanted these adolescents to become Street Dreams soldiers . . . and we wanted to work ourselves out of a job. We taught the kids to take over our roles and become community organizers, because that's what teamwork is all about: teaching your skills to other, younger people so they can move on up.

We saw these beaten-down youngsters grow in confidence in front of our eyes. We had kids wanting to be woodworkers, to get into HR, to teach dance: all sorts! They came to us dysfunctional and unengaged, and grew so confident that they began empowering other young people. That was cool to see.

Jade and I were a great team and the Street Dreams kids knew that we were on their side. They knew we had their backs. A lot of them came from broken homes, and Jade and I probably became a bit of a surrogate family for them. And that made it all the sadder, for everyone, when that family fell apart.

When Jade and I split up, our Street Dream soldiers suffered like any poor kids do when their parents separate. They knew there were tensions between us. I could see them thinking: *Do I go with Jay, or with Jade?* It was proper heart-breaking, and

I think the feeling of guilt it gave me contributed to my breakdown.

Teamwork and team spirit are precious but they depend on trust, and when that trust goes, the teamwork goes with it. People who had felt part of a family or a community, suddenly feel very alone and unprotected. And I'm sure you don't need *me* to tell you that that can be the loneliest feeling in the world.

After my marriage ended, I didn't feel part of any team at all. I felt totally on my own. I've had that grim feeling at a few points in my life, but this was the worst it had ever been. I'd never felt so low, or so lost: *literally* lost, as I ended up sitting in that random car park for days, having forgotten who, and what, I was.

It takes a lot to recover from a breakdown like that and I did it by finding a new team; a new family. My friend Gerald Bailey encouraged me to live with his mum and dad, Thelma and Cass, in Wolverhampton, and he couldn't have done a smarter thing, or saved my life in a better way. They coaxed me back to life.

Thelma was like the best mum that any boy could wish for, and Cass . . . well, Cass was the dad that I had never had. They took me into their home, broken, and they fed me, watered me, looked after me and gave me love. From the day I met them, I knew that they were totally on my side.

It was teamwork. It was community. It was *family*. Thelma and Cass cared for me and supported me in my hour of need. They never said, 'We've got you, Jay,' but they didn't *need* to.

I could sense it every time I looked at them. I *knew* they were totally on my side.

It helped me to rebuild and recover. It came naturally to them, mainly because they are great people, but also because I think it is something the Caribbean community are good at. They – or I think I can say *we*, because I can count myself in there – care for each other and look out for each other. We know how to be one big support network.

When you think about it, a lot of the older West Indian expats in Britain now, the *Windrush* generation, are on their own. They've lost their partners and they may not have any family members left to speak of. If we're not careful, they can feel like they're totally alone – like I did before my crack-up.

For these old-timers, their community is the corner shop or the post office. They might go to the same market stall every day and only buy a couple of spuds, but have a good chinwag with the stall-holder. That's where they get what we in the Caribbean community call their 'flowers'. Where they're part of something.

It's what teamwork is all about and, for me, it's a proper crucial life lesson we can all learn, whatever our own situation might be. *Community is everything*. And it's an ongoing process. In fact, here's another handy little saying for you:

'Coming together is the beginning. Keeping together is progress. Working together is success.'

Because, believe you me, you've got to work at togetherness and teamwork. It doesn't just happen on its own! Teams work best when they all share the same goals and keep striving every day to achieve those goals. And that's the truest of all in the most intimate team of all: a partnership. A marriage.

Anybody who's been through a divorce doesn't want ever to go through another one. So, when they find themselves in another relationship, they do everything they can to keep it happy and healthy, and stop it from falling apart. And, to me, that means putting certain ground rules and strategies in place.

I got married again, in 2022, to Lisa, whom I call Tiny (I'm sure she won't mind me telling you that – well, I hope not, anyway!). I love her to bits, and I'm looking to spend the rest of my life with her. She feels the same so, as far as I'm concerned, it's the job of the two of us to make that happen.

No relationship is perfect – even newlyweds! Lisa and I argue every now and then, like every couple since Adam and Eve. But we never start shouting about splitting up, or about getting divorced. Instead, we have a framework in place that lets us settle any arguments happily and move on.

If Tiny and I are having a barney, we have a rule that the person who is not talking has to listen. I mean, *really* listen. We never butt in, or interrupt one another. We listen closely and then, if the other person stops talking, we ask, 'Are you done?'

Lisa might *not* be done. She might have more to say, and then she can continue and I can't say any more until she's properly finished. But then when she *is* done, and she says she is, it is my role to go up to her and give her a great big hug. And she'll do the same to me, if it's the other way round.

Here's what we do. We say the magic words – 'Are you done?' – and then we step forward and we embrace. We hug each other, and we don't let go of that hug until we've both said that we love each other. It's a lesson we've learned on how to move forwards: as partners, as a relationship and as a *team*.

I mean, what's the alternative? Holding on to the anger and the argument so that it festers inside you? *No, thank you!* I'd rather say, 'Tiny, I didn't like what you did, and it made me feel bad, but I love you like mad so now let's move on.' I mean, we're both trying to achieve the same thing: being happy together.

There's another little saying I put on my socials: 'Showing your weakness allows others to show their strength in supporting you.' And I think there is a lot of truth in that. Because being part of a team involves, first of all, being strong enough to admit that you need help.

'Showing your weakness allows others to show their strength in supporting you.'

Some people, especially blokes, can't admit that they need help from anybody. They think of themselves as lone wolves, tough guys, who can handle whatever the world throws at them on their own. They hate showing what they think of as 'weakness' in any way at all.

The irony is that showing that weakness would bring them support and comfort. Think about when you lose a family member. What's the point in trying to tough it out? It's when you're looking down, or you're in tears, that somebody will throw an arm around your shoulder. That's when you get the love you need.

As I say, teamwork, and community, are everything. They show you that you're not alone in this world: *we're all in this together*. And, of course, the biggest, and most public, team that I am involved in now, and have been since 2017, is *The Repair Shop*.

I've got to be honest here. I knew *The Repair Shop* was going to be special the very first time I walked in the door of that workshop all those years ago. I could sense we were going to be a super-close-knit team, and that we were going to do a lot of working, playing and laughing together. *Well, you can say that again!*

Every team needs a shared purpose, and it was obvious what ours was from day one: a love for heritage crafts. We all shared a passion for craftsmen's skills from years gone by, and for using those special skills to restore damaged antiques and heirlooms to their beautiful original condition.

We were all dedicated restorers but we didn't know each other's trades. I was a furniture upholsterer, but I knew zilch about metalworking, or how to fix ceramics or clocks. I loved walking around the workshop, asking Dom or Steve questions:

'What are you doing, mate?' Or, often: 'Wow, how did you just do *that*?'

Teamwork works best when everybody is on the same page. On *The Repair Shop* we're all reading from the same book. It's not like when you start a new school as a child, and you have to find common ground with the other kids to make friends. We all had common ground from the off.

It makes us a natural team. One of the nicest things about *The Repair Shop* is that sometimes the restorers all work together. A lady might bring in a gorgeous old grandfather clock. 'Steve, can you get it ticking again?' I'll ask. 'Will, can you bring the wood back to life? And Dom, mate, can you get the clock hands shining so I can see my face in them?'

Teamwork. *Community*. It's what *The Repair Shop*, and life, is all about.

Life never stands still, and, of course, my role on *The Repair Shop* changed a lot when the producers asked me to stop being the upholsterer fixing the chairs, and to begin presenting the show. Suddenly, I was no longer 'just' a team member but a foreman, ordering the rest of them around!

I was happy with the change, because greeting the guests and chatting with them about their items suits my skillset. Although my introvert side means I need time to myself, I'm a people person and I love talking, and listening. I still feel just as much a part of *The Repair Shop* team as ever. I just have a slightly different role than the one I used to do.

For me, that's how life is. Your teams will change sometimes and your role within them will alter. You will gain members and lose others. In your family, kids will grow up and leave home. New people will marry into the family. The important thing? You stay committed to the family, whatever happens.

Let's face it, most people are involved in more than one team day-to-day. There's your work, with friends and colleagues. Your family, with your loved ones that you are closest to. Your community: the people you live next to and interact with. And all of these teams make you feel that you *belong*: that you have a place.

I'm no different. As well as *The Repair Shop*, and my TV production company, and life at home with Lisa, I have Jay & Co. It's my furniture restoration company that I started back in 2015, both to bring damaged beautiful vintage furniture back to life and to train disadvantaged young people in a fascinating trade.

Jay & Co is my baby, my labour of love, but as I've got busier and busier with *The Repair Shop*, my TV career and even stuff like writing books (!) nowadays, I've had to take more of a back seat in the company and delegate a lot more. That's fine, because I've got a great team.

I'm still very involved in Jay & Co. When I'm not filming on *The Repair Shop*, you'll usually find me in a corner of the workshop on a Zoom or Skype call with one of my worker bees there. We'll be deep in discussion: should we buy *this* chair?

What can we do with *that* one? Does *this* design work, and *this* colour?

I love doing all that – I probably talk to the Jay & Co crew more than I do to Lisa! – but, at the same time, I trust the people I have working there. I trust their vision and their hands-on ability, and I'm happy to leave a lot of big decisions to them. I have faith in them because I know we're a great team.

'The nice thing about teamwork is that you always have people on your side.'

Some people set up companies and try to do everything themselves. Maybe even *I* was like that when I started out, but you know what? You keep trying to do that for too long and you'll soon be cream-crackered! No, you need to employ good people, trust them, and allow them to do their jobs! *Bosh!*

And there's the point: the life lesson that is really worth learning. 'The nice thing about teamwork is that you always have people on your side.' And once you've got a fantastic team in place, you can relax, stop stressing and get on with enjoying the good things in life. You know it makes sense . . .

6

RACISM

'A man can't ride your back unless it's bent'

I pick up my pearls of wisdom from here, there and everywhere. All over the shop! Some of them, I dream up myself. Others, I might hear or see while I'm out and about and think, *Yeah! I love that!* And a few of them are direct quotations from some of the greatest figures in history.

It was Martin Luther King who said 'A man can't ride your back unless it's bent.' I didn't really know who MLK was when I was a kid. I just knew his name, and that he was significant to the Black community, like Nelson Mandela and Bob Marley. It was only as I grew older that I realized quite how important he was.

I want to say something here. This book of life lessons is

for everybody, no matter your age, skin colour, background or gender. It's not aimed at any one demographic. At the same time, you pick up life lessons through your learned experience, and my own experience was as a Black kid growing up in Hackney in the seventies and eighties.

And, sad though it is, that meant racism.

What did Martin Luther King mean by that quote? To me, he was saying: don't be negative, no matter what kind of attack you're under. Stand proud. I make sure, every day, that my back is straight, my shoulders are up, I look smart and nobody is going to ride on me and weigh me down. And you should do the same.

'A man can't ride your back unless it's bent.'

I first met racism at secondary school, but unknown to me, my mum, aunties and uncles were protecting me from it even before then. There was a group of elders who'd get together to fight off the local skinheads and Mods and Rockers to keep them from coming on to our estate to find us kids and cause us harm.

I never knew anything about that, but I certainly got to know about people who hated the colour of my skin as soon as I got to secondary school. As I said in my life story, *Making It*, the name-calling and the insults in the playground started almost from my first day there. And then came the violence.

When you're eleven years old, and don't really know what's

going on, it's hard to know how to react to being racially bullied. I tried doing all of the correct things. I went and told the teachers, but they didn't want to know. Weren't interested. I tried talking nicely to the big kids who were slapping me about, but where did that get me?

'Can you give me my pencil case back, please?'

'Shut up, you little wog!'

'Will you stop hitting me?'

'Fuck off, you Black bastard! Go back to where you came from!'

It was horrible and painful and stupid, and I soon saw that I couldn't talk to these thugs, or reason with them. They didn't want any communication. All they knew was abuse and violence. I realized the only option I had to defend myself was to hit back, to be violent myself, and so that was the option I took.

It wasn't just in school. When I used to walk down the street as a teenager, I'd get proper nasty comments. As I said earlier, the police would pull us into their vans and give us a kicking. We'd go into another local area, like Islington, and the shop-keepers didn't want to treat us nicely, or even to serve us.

How do you pull life lessons from experiences like that? What is there to learn? Well, one thing I picked up is something that is just as relevant today, to any kids of *any* colour who might be going through the same ordeal. Like Martin Luther King said: Stand tall. Don't let yourself be defined by bigots and their prejudices.

And *prejudice* was what it was. I'd hear someone say they didn't like Black people because one of them had robbed his house, or mugged his mate. Well, so what? There were lots of White people going around robbing houses and doing muggings – did he hate all White people as a consequence, as well? No! Do me a favour!

As a hot-headed young kid, the unfairness of racism and prejudice can eat you up and consume you. You spend a lot of time *angry*, which is what I did. It's only as you get older, and a bit wiser, that you realize that is a waste of energy. It's totally negative emotion, and you just don't need it in your life.

Looking back, it was when I went to work at the homeless hostel, at twenty-one, that I started to get rid of all that negativity. I realized that if someone made a racist comment to me, I didn't have to put it in my rucksack to bend my back all day. Why should I? It didn't *belong* to me. It wasn't my problem. It was theirs.

I didn't twig overnight because it's not an easy process. But I began to understand the value of those Martin Luther King words: 'A man can't ride your back unless it's bent.' I learned that you can stand high, and proud, and tell yourself: 'Ignore it. I am what I am. I know I'm a good person. Those haters don't know me.'

When I went to university, I learned more about the history of racism and how long it had been endemic in Britain. I'd always assumed anti-Black racism was a recent phenomenon.

It was an eye-opener for me, and not in a good way, to learn that it was a systemic problem that stretched back for decades and more.

The funny – if that's the word – thing is that even among the educated students at university, I met some racism! I got quite friendly with a White lad on my course. He always seemed OK, so I was surprised when a few of my Black and Asian mates came to me and said they wanted to give him a good beating.

'Why are you mates with that wanker, Jay?' they asked me. 'He says bad shit – he's always using the N-word and the P-word! We're going to sort him out!'

'Now, hold up!' I said. 'Before you start getting violent, give me a chance to have a word with him. He seems a good lad to me. Maybe he doesn't know what he is saying?'

I spoke to the geezer and that was exactly what it was. He had grown up in a tiny village of 300 people in Norfolk, where everybody was White. As a kid, he'd heard those words all the time, and he was just repeating what he'd heard. When I told him how it made our fellow students feel, he was well upset.

'Shit, Jay, I never meant to do that!' he said. 'It's just the names I'm used to using. I'll stop it – of course I'll stop it!'

It was an important exchange. His 'racism' was unintentional: ignorance, not malice. He changed his behaviour and he was fine after that. In fact, he ended up getting married to a woman of colour. I believe his family disowned him at first when he did that, but everything is fine now and he's very happy.

To me, there is a major life lesson there. *Don't judge people too quickly*. That guy was being ignorant, but that was all he knew, coming from where he did. In that particular situation I felt able to communicate with him: I explained, he listened and understood, and he changed his ways. Everyone was a winner!

When I left university, and I started doing the Street Dreams project with Jade, I felt a lot more clued in about racism and how to survive it. I thought I had learned a few life lessons myself, and I wanted to share them with the young people that we were working with who might also be going through what I had.

I'd say to these kids: 'Racism is *always* going to be there. I don't like it, you don't like it, but it is what it is. You might be Black, Asian, whatever – you can still suffer from it. The question is, how are you going to deal with it?' And the answer is to flip a negative attitude to a positive one.

'I like to think of racism as being like a door,' I'd say. 'You can ask, "Why is it like this? Why has it got a handle?" You can drive yourself crazy thinking about that door, and why it is there, or you can just walk through it, get to the other side and move on. And I know which one I'd rather do!'

While I was at uni, I wrote a dissertation called *Manufacturing a Black Criminal*. It was well deep. It argued that our society is set up in a way that drives Black youth towards crime. Some of the Black kids I mentored at Street Dreams had already been

in trouble with the law. So, I explained my theory – my thesis
– to them.

'There's this old saying that crime doesn't pay,' I said to
them. 'But it's not true, because it does.'

'Huh? What do you mean, Jay?' they'd ask.

'Crime *does* pay,' I'd say. 'It just doesn't pay for *you*!' They
would look puzzled, so I'd go into greater depth.

'Think about it. If you break into a car, you'll get nicked by
two police constables. They'll be on about £30,000 each: £60,000
in total. They take you to the station and you get booked in by
the duty sergeant. He'll be on a bit more: maybe £40,000. *Bosh!*
We're up to £100,000 already!

'You get seen by the duty solicitor, who is probably also on
£40,000. You go to court, or to magistrates' court. The people
who deal with you there will be on at least £100,000 between
them. Are you keeping count? We're up to more than £200,000
by now, just for the crime that you've committed!

'Then you go to prison. You've got prison warders, victim
support, social workers, all that infrastructure. It costs the government about £45,000 to put you in prison for a year. Plus, if you've
broken into the car in my street, my insurance premiums go up.
So, insurance companies make money off your criminal activity!'

Sometimes, the Street Dreams kids would butt in and tell me
that they hated the police, or social workers, or the authorities
in general. I would hear them out, and then I'd tell them:

'OK. You don't like those people. But you're keeping them

in a job by committing crime! It's because of *you* that they can have their house in a nice area, and have two cars, and go on holidays, and their kids can go to private schools. It's all paid for off the back of your criminality! You're financing it!

'Imagine if there was no crime. There'd be no need for police, or court, or prisons. *You* are keeping all of those institutions in business with your attitude and your actions!'

I would say this to them, and with the vast majority of the kids I said it to, I could see their brains whirring as they took it all in. **'Don't be a stereotype. Don't be a caricature.'** Sometimes, their mouths might even drop open in shock. 'Shit, Jay, you're right!' they'd say. They wouldn't look best pleased about it, but you know what? Some life lessons are tough to learn.

I guess not everyone is going to agree with what I'm saying here. A few of you might be shaking your head as you read this: 'Hang on, you've lost me here, Jay!' But to me, what I'm saying is as plain as the nose on my face. And it leads me into another very important life lesson for young people of colour today. Which is: 'Don't be a stereotype. Don't be a caricature.' Because the way young Black people are represented in the media nowadays, in movies and TV and adverts, is exactly that. Those representations don't give a good example to the youth, but it's easy for impressionable kids to want to follow them.

What do I mean? Well, I just watched an ad for a trainer store the other day. It was all young Black kids: either running fast, or with their trousers hanging down low. It just projected a complete caricature: that all Black people are only good at sport and like to wear sportswear.

As a role model, and as a life lesson, it's not a good one, and it's not one that kids of *any* colour should be soaking up. And you know what? It's not even correct. Because, going about my daily life, I've met people of colour who have achieved so much in their lives that they would blow your bloody socks off.

I can introduce you to a British Black guy whose IQ has been measured as higher than Albert Einstein's. I know Britain's first blind Black lawyer. I can introduce you to two guys who brought out new software that took computer tech to another level, then sold their tech company for billions. *They're* the guys to admire *as well* as sports pros and musicians.

I used to tell my Street Dreams kids: 'Look at music. Why do so many Black artists sing, or rap, about degrading their own race, or shooting each other, or how badly they treat women? Why do we do this?'

It's the life lesson I learned at university, again: it's *manufacturing*. White bosses control the music industry and put this music out. Even back in 1991, *Newsweek* magazine did a cover story on gangsta rap that revealed that eighty per cent – *eighty per cent!* – of the people who buy that music are White. And it caricatures and damages people of colour.

Now I'm on the telly, and I've got a certain profile, I share life lessons such as this whenever I can with kids to try to keep them on the straight and narrow. Because, some would argue, it's a short step from them admiring gangsta rap videos to trying to join gangs, deal weed or get hold of knives or guns themselves.

I try to help but it can be hard because so many young people of colour don't want to listen. They have got no interest in anything I've got to say. Why? Because my voice isn't nearly as loud as the rap music and videos and the trainer ads.

Teenagers look at me, if they see me at all, and I don't fit the image of what they want to be. I haven't got a bad attitude, and my trousers aren't hanging down low. My trousers are pulled up, I'm smartly dressed and polite and positive, and I think they just decide that I'm a coconut: brown on the outside but white on the inside.

I've been told that the kids think I'm not 'keeping it real', whatever that bloody means, and so they're not interested. I'll give you a for instance. When *Making It* came out and I did my signing tour of bookshops, I must have signed a thousand copies of the book. Do you know how many of those were for Black people? *Four*.

Well, it is what it is. One life lesson I've learned over the years is that you can't change the world overnight. All I can do is keep slogging away, day by day, trying to get my message across. I can put my little positive, inspirational messages up on my socials . . . and I can keep inviting people to my Sunday School.

'Communication is key to everything.'

What's my Sunday School? It's a weekend thing I do on my social media where I highlight Black figures who have contributed to British history: people like Mary Seacole, the nurse in the Crimean war, Professor Stuart Hall, the sociologist, and Sean Levey, the first Black jockey to ride in the Epsom Derby horse race.

I like to just put the information out in a matter-of-fact way, no pressure, no chip on my shoulder. Aggression turns people off – and, as I said earlier, the important thing in life is to keep communicating.

There's that life lesson again: 'Communication is key to everything.' I don't want to shout at racist people. If I met a racist today, face-to-face, I'd like to sit down with them and have a chat so I could try to understand where their beliefs come from. I'd like to listen to them, and them to me.

That's important because, ultimately a deep-seated problem like racism can only be solved by communication. I appreciated Black Lives Matter when it became more widely known about but, ultimately, I think it was just a hashtag to a lot of people. The same with taking the knee at football matches: the conversation we needed to have around it never happened.

The debate around racism isn't static. It's always shifting and changing. The funny thing is that sometimes well-meaning people come along and they try to move the conversation on and promote inclusivity and, inadvertently, they can end up making things worse.

A few years ago, this new acronym appeared: BAME, or

Black Asian and Minority Ethnic. The idea was to make society more inclusive of people from those racial backgrounds, but I don't know one member of the Black community, one person of colour, who liked the term. In fact, it pissed everybody I know right off.

Why? Because they didn't want just to be lumped into one clumsy category. Some people are South Asian. Some are East Asian. Others would prefer to be categorized as 'African Caribbean'. There are so many different racial categories within 'BAME' and a one-size-fits-all title like that just doesn't wash.

Of course, it's important to bear in mind that while 'BAME' is a mistake, it is a *well-intentioned* mistake. It's not a racist phrase, because somebody or other dreamed it up as a way of trying to *fight* racism. But rather than invent categories, society needs to think of all people of colour as exactly that: *people*. Individuals.

So, what's all this doing in my book of life lessons? Easy: as a Black man, these are big lessons I have learned in my life, often the hard way, and I'd like to help young people of colour to accrue the same wisdom. It can be a hard road, but it's one we all have to walk down.

Ultimately, it all comes back to that Martin Luther King quote: 'A man can't ride your back unless it's bent.' Hold your head up high, keep your shoulders back, and remember that you came from kings and queens. Respect yourself. And only *then* can we stop getting angry at history and start talking about positive Black futures.

7

POSITIVITY

'Be willing to be a beginner every single morning'

Most people don't like to think of themselves as beginners. They believe they've picked up enough suss and know-how at whatever they're doing to have moved on from that novice stage. Well, I say the exact opposite: we should all be willing to be a beginner every single morning.

I'm not joking! I mean it! Each morning, when we wake up, we should be like a kid on Christmas Day: wide-eyed and excited about what lies ahead. We should see every day as a new beginning, a clean slate, a chance to go out and make our mark on the world. Because, if we don't, what's the point in waking up at all?!

What do I mean by being a beginner? I mean seeing the

world through fresh eyes and keeping an open mind to it. I mean waking up and trying new things, rather than expecting the day to be exactly the same as the day before, and the day before that. Because, you know what? If that's all you expect, that's all you'll get!

I imagine a few of you readers will be rolling your eyes at this – 'Come on! Get real, Jay!' – but bear with me on this one. I know we all wake up and we have stuff we have to do. We have to go to work. We have to get the kids off to school. We all have our first-thing routines – but don't let them become mindless rituals.

Here's what you can do. Do you set the alarm for 7 a.m. each day to give you time to have a shower, breakfast and get to work? Well, why not go to bed earlier the night before and set it for 6 a.m. now and then? You can have an extra hour to swan about, meditate, read a book – whatever you want! Get some 'you' time!

Or do you mooch into the bathroom in your pyjamas at the same time every day, like most people, and stand in the same place to brush your teeth? Try going in a bit earlier and standing in a different spot! Brush them with your left hand rather than your right! They're little things, but they can jolt you out of your dull routine.

This might all sound trivial to you, but for me it's an important life lesson. We can all vary our daily rituals and mix things up a bit. It makes us focus more on what we are doing, and why we are doing it. It's exercise for the mind, and it makes us that little bit sharper and more aware. It freshens us up.

The way we start each day has a major influence on what that day will be like. It shapes our subconscious thinking. So, it's good to make sure you're wide awake. I like to start the day by dropping down and doing a few press-ups to get my body moving and get myself ready to rock 'n' roll.

Well, I say I *like* to do that – you wouldn't think so, to look at me! Some days, I get out of bed and I'll do anything to delay getting down on the floor to do those damn press-ups! I'll prevaricate like mad: *What's that tissue doing on the table? I'll put it over THERE! No, over HERE! I know, let's have a look out of the window . . .*

'When a new day begins, challenge yourself to smile genuinely and gratefully.'

I'll procrastinate for a few minutes but then I'll take a deep breath, do the press-ups, and you know what? I always feel better for doing them afterwards. *Always*. And the point is, don't let the press-ups become a routine either. Some mornings, do sit-ups instead. Or squats. Mix it up. It will keep giving you a new perspective.

Keeping that morning energy going, here's another saying that I like: 'When a new day begins, challenge yourself to smile genuinely and gratefully.' Because if you wake up with a smile on your face, it can last all day. And, if one thing is certain, it is that negative energy will never give you a positive life.

Negativity will always attract negativity. It's just the way it is. For me, you can't get a positive from a negative. This isn't the nicest saying in this book, and pardon the expression, but if you stay around shit long enough, eventually it doesn't seem to smell. Why is that? Because you get used to it! And that's no way to live.

Pointless negativity does my head in. It's just the way I've always been. I'll give you an example. The other day, I was at a furniture event for Jay & Co and I got talking to a major company owner. He's a big player in the British furniture industry – but all that was coming out of him was negativity.

'The furniture business in the UK has a problem with success,' he told me. 'They can't handle it. They have a problem with failure as well. They like mediocrity and safe stuff, so that is all that we end up with. I'm totally fed up with it.'

I was finding this conversation a bit depressing, so I challenged the geezer. 'Do *you* have a problem with success?' I asked him.

'No.'

'Do *you* have a problem with failure?'

'No.'

'So, what are *you* doing for the future of the furniture industry?' I asked. 'You're respected in this game. Why not show a bit of positivity, instead of this negativity you're spitting out? Isn't that your responsibility?'

A group of people had gathered around us by now, and I

could see them looking surprised, because this guy is a proper big cheese and he'd probably never been challenged like that before. I could see the thought bubbles forming over their heads: *Blimey! How is he going to deal with this one?*

The company owner looked at me and I could see he wasn't sure how to answer. So, I told him: 'I'm going to leave that with you. I'm going to come back to you in two years, and if you've done nothing you're going to have to shut up, because I don't deal in negativity and you're just stood here talking negative.

'I'm trying to reintroduce some life into the furniture industry,' I went on. 'I am attempting new things. You're respected but you're just talking everyone down. You hold the future of the furniture business in your hands, mate, and you need to start doing something different!'

What was nice was that the guy broke into a smile, nodded and shook my hand. I took his business card. 'I'm on your case!' I laughed. 'If you haven't done anything in two years, I'll find you again and I'll rip this card up. I won't want to know you!' 'OK, you've got a deal!' the geezer grinned back.

And there's the major life lesson. If you surround yourself with negativity, you get to the point where you don't even know that you're being negative. That whole way of thinking just *becomes* you. Well, I'm allergic to that manner of thinking. If I get the chance, I'll *always* try to find the positive in any situation.

I was trying to explain that to a group of young people I

was talking to the other day. I said to them, 'Even if I stub my toe, and it hurts for a minute, I try to see that as a positive.'

'Eh? What you on about?' one girl asked me. 'You've stubbed your toe and you're saying "Ouch!" and holding your foot! How can *that* be positive?'

'Well, maybe I wasn't meant to take the next step I was about to take!' I said. 'I might have stepped into the road and got run over by a bus! It all happens for a reason!'

'Wow!' she said. 'I'd never thought of it *that* way before . . .'

'Well, it's about time you started!'

Being willing to be a beginner every day means being prepared to do new things you've never attempted previously. I don't mean that you have to go sky-diving, or take up pole-vaulting! Just look at everyday things, your day-to-day life, from a different viewpoint from how you normally see them. Try some fresh thinking.

Look at when you go off on summer holiday. You go some-where completely new and unknown, escape your routine, and come back refreshed and revitalized. Yet you don't have to jet off to the sun to do that. You can do it just as effectively at home or at work. You just need a bit of lateral thinking.

I've got a friend who is a lawyer. She was moaning to me recently that she spends all day in the courtroom. She takes sandwiches in with her, and eats them sitting at her desk. Then, at night, she goes home with her head full of the cases that she is working on. She feels like her whole life is about work.

'Well, why don't you take a little holiday?' I asked her.

'I haven't got time for a holiday, Jay!' she said. 'I've got too many cases!'

'I don't mean go away,' I answered. 'You get a lunch break, don't you?'

'Yeah.'

'Treat that as your holiday! Don't sit at your desk. Go to a restaurant, or a cafe. See a different environment. Sit in the park and jot down notes on what you can see, or take a photo. That's a memory and it will let you think about something else other than work.'

My mate looked well sceptical, but she said she'd give it a go. Next time I saw her, a few weeks later, she looked a load happier. 'You were right, Jay!' she laughed. 'I didn't think it would work, but it's made a real difference!'

Where do I find this energy to bounce out of bed each morning as if every day is a new beginning? I've always been a bit that way, it's just my nature, but – and this might sound strange to you – I think it's been even more the case since I had my breakdown. I feel like I've appreciated life even more ever since then.

Why should that be? Well, when you've hit rock bottom to the point that you're trying to find a motorway bridge to drive into, and you manage to bounce back from that, *every day is a bonus*. You're simply grateful to be alive. It gives you a whole valuable new outlook.

I had never been lower in my life than I was when I had my breakdown and I went missing, but going through that low, and surviving it, gave me a total new lease of life. Falling down and mending myself made me so strong that now I really *do* feel like I'm beginning again every morning. I'm lucky: it's a superpower!

Everybody feels down at times, and even if it's not as bad a crisis as mine was, a great life lesson is knowing how to pick yourself back up. My favourite way is music. The trick is to play your most loved songs, the ones that make you want to dance as if nobody is looking – and then to do exactly that.

Boom! The effect that can have on your spirits is amazing. Music has this trick of being so infectious that it moves your body and your mind. You know how little toddlers grin and wave their arms when they hear a song they love? It can do the same for us. It can get you moving even if you're the worst dancer in the world.*

We all have special tunes to lift us out of the doldrums. My go-to song is 'Do I Do' by Stevie Wonder. There's a really long version where Stevie goes proper nuts, and it is magical. Nina Simone can do it for me, as well. 'Sinnerman' is amazing and so is 'Good Bait'. Instant happiness!

This book is full of inspirational phrases that I love. Well, just for a change, here is one that I hate. It's a cynical old saying

---

* Anybody who saw me on the *Strictly Come Dancing* 2021 Christmas Special, please don't comment, lol!

hat is the exact opposite of everything I believe, and I wince every time I hear somebody saying it: 'You can't teach an old dog new tricks.'

Ouch! I'm sorry, and excuse my language again, but that is absolute bollocks! You can *always* learn new tricks. It's not a question of age: it's attitude. You can be a young person, in your twenties, and behaving like an 'old dog' in that you're stuck in a boring rut every day and are not able to change. Or you can be a much older person who is excited to try new things and engage with change. Look at the 'silver surfers': the pensioners who have mastered the internet and learned to enjoy social media. If they're mangy old mutts, what are they doing having fun online, eh?

No, you can pick up new tricks whatever age you are. I'm happy to say that I'm still learning stuff all the time. I suppose I've been on TV for a while now but it still feels like a new world for me – *like I'm still beginning* – and I absorb new bits of knowledge, information and language every day.

There again, I don't always know what it is that I'm being told! I will be on the set of *The Repair Shop* and some person I've never met will come bounding up to me, shake my hand and introduce themselves.

'Hi!' they'll say. 'I'm a new AP!' Or: 'I'm an SP!'

I'll stare at them blankly. Sometimes, I might even take my cap off and scratch my noggin.

'Hello!' I'll reply. 'Nice to meet you, but what's that when it's at home, then?'

'I'm an associate producer!' they'll say. Or: 'A serie producer!'

'OK, great! Well, that's your title, but what does it *mean* What do you *do?*' And the funny thing is, half the time, they can't explain it. They can tell me their job title, but not wha their actual role is.

'If you don't know, don't be afraid to ask.'

It's just industry jargon, really It's easy to hide behind that jargo – except that, for me, it's not. As dyslexic person, I need to know wha it means, because it is confusing fo me if I don't understand. In fact, if the person doesn't tell m what they actually *do*, I tend not to store their title in my memory bank.

You know what? I'll think to myself. *I don't know what you title means, and nor do YOU seem to, so what's the point in remem bering it? I've got more important stuff to be thinking about . . .*

There's a great life lesson in there: 'If you don't know, don't be afraid to ask.' I went on a business course once, and the guy giving

'There is no such thing as a silly question.'

the course said, 'There is no such thing as a silly question.' Le me tell you, I thought that was one of the best things I eve heard.

Why? Well, a lot of people are scared to ask a question i case they look silly: *Oh, I'll look daft if I ask that! I'll go awa and Google it later!* But if they don't ask, they won't get what's going on. They'll probably say something inappropriate and end up looking much sillier than if they'd asked in the first place.

So, if you don't understand something, go for the jugular. Come straight out with it: 'What do you mean by that? What does that word mean?' Be like a kid. It doesn't matter what age you are; you can still say: 'I don't get it. Can you explain it to me?' That's what I do, and it works.

A guy that I work with showed me a piece in *The Guardian* newspaper a while back. It was a nice review of my *Jay Blades: Learning to Read at 51* TV show, and it said, 'Jay Blades seems to be constitutionally incapable of flannel.' 'That's good, isn't it?' the guy asked me.

'I don't know!' I replied. 'What does it mean?'

The bloke explained that 'flannel' means waffle and not getting to the point, and I laughed and agreed that, yeah, that *was* a good comment about me. There is so much flannel in everyday life – especially working in television! – and I can't be doing with it. I like to cut the crap and know what's going on.

If you're willing to be a beginner every single morning, and to look at the world through fresh eyes every day, you're receptive to special things that you might otherwise miss. Here's a nice one for you: 'Everything has beauty, but not everyone sees it.'

I love that saying. Why? Because it's so simple and so true! And the sentiment it expresses is obvious: there is so much beauty around us, everywhere, every single second. All we have to learn to do is to take note of it.

'Everything has beauty, but not everyone sees it.' We are all so busy going about our day-to-day lives that we don't look up and we don't look forward. We don't look at the buildings, we don't notice the sky, and we don't smell the flowers. You might walk past an amazing tree each morning and not even see it. It's all *head-down-and-rush-rush-rush*.

There are many things I love about going to Barbados to visit my mum, and one is that everyone in the street smiles and says, 'Good morning!' or 'Good afternoon!' Man, it makes such a difference to the day! I've sometimes tried doing it myself in the UK. Depending on where I am, people can be surprised – but they like it.

I was filming in the street in London the other day and a woman walked past in a gorgeous long coat. I said, 'That's a beautiful coat!' and she gave me a radiant smile as she went by. Little gestures and comments like that can make people so happy, so why not say them? It's a really cool thing to do!

'Stop racing around everywhere. Learn to stop and smell the flowers.' You know what? I can't think of many more vital life lessons than that. And it leads me to another smart life hack, along the same lines: 'Doing nothing brings everything into perspective.'

'Stop racing around everywhere. Learn to stop and smell the flowers.'

Now, don't take this the wrong way! I don't mean it's a good thing to be a couch potato, sitting on your arse all day, with the TV remote glued to your hand: 'It's OK, Jay said I can go on the dole!'

Ha! No, I'm saying something that is hopefully a lot more philosophical.

What I mean is sometimes, just now and then, *stop dead and do nothing*. Break away from your emails, and your social media, and stand still. Or lie down, if you want to. Look around you. Take it all in. Re-centre yourself and get back in touch with where you are. *Appreciate being alive.*

None of us is going to be here forever. Death gets all of us, eventually. So, while you're breathing in and out, are active and healthy, and lucky enough to be able to walk around, enjoy life. Be grateful. Be willing to be a beginner every day and it will remind you how amazing it is to be alive. Really!

'Doing nothing brings everything into perspective.'

Sometimes, I bump into people and they ask, 'You all right, Jay? How are you doing?'

'I'm alive,' I answer. 'And that's the main thing.'

It might sound well morbid to them, and they look surprised: 'Eh? That's a bit strong, innit?'

'No,' I grin back. 'Because as long as I am alive, I can do the work that I need to do and I can achieve what I want to achieve!'

And there's the moral of the tale, for me. Never forget that we're here to achieve, and to move forward. And the more we do that, the more it will put a smile on our faces when we wake up for the first time every single morning.

8

REACHING OUT

*'Use your influence to change those who are not like you.
That's how we make real change'*

This book is based on inspirational phrases that I have gathered over the months and years, and yet not everything in life is so positive. There are times that I have myself a gander at social media sites, and they don't exactly look very social. In fact, they look like a warzone.

I don't think you need me to tell you that society is very divided right now. There are all sorts of arguments going on, about politics and racism and sexism, and transgender rights, but not a lot of *debate*. It seems like as soon as someone puts their head up with an unpopular opinion, they get shut down right away.

I'll give you a for-instance of how nasty it can get. An older woman I know was in an online chatgroup not so long ago. Because she didn't know any better, she used the word 'coloured' – 'I have a lot of coloured friends,' she said. And *bosh!* The cancel police of the internet were on her like a ton of bricks!

'You can't use that word!' they told her. 'That's racist! *You're* a racist!' Now, this lady isn't *any* kind of racist. Obviously, these insults upset her, so she defended herself, doubled down and fired a few choice words of her own off at the people who were attacking her. Then she came to me for advice.

'I don't know what I did wrong, Jay!' she said. 'I didn't mean to offend anybody. Why were they so angry?'

I wanted to help, so I explained the history of the word. 'White people invented it because they used to think that Black people look as if we've been "coloured in",' I said. 'They thought being White was "normal" and anything else looked weird.

'It's funny, in a way!' I laughed. 'Black people *don't* change colour. White people go red when they're angry, blue when they're cold, and brown when they've been in the sun, so *they're* the ones that are "colouring"! But, joking aside, it's a phrase that has got some bad connotations, and it can offend people.'

My friend listened closely and then she said, 'OK. Now you've explained it, Jay, I can see not to use that word. I get it. I didn't get it last night because the people in the chatgroup didn't explain it to me – they only shouted "Racist!!" It was just confrontation, confrontation, confrontation!'

And that, right there, is the problem.

The internet rules the world today and social media appears to be at the centre of so many people's lives. We spend a lot of time on our socials, and if we are to spend that time arguing and name-calling, that's not good for our well-being or mental health. That's why this chapter's sub-title is an important lesson: 'Use your influence to change those who are not like you. That's how we make real change.'

It's simple. If you see someone on social media saying something you don't agree with – on politics, race, sexuality, whatever – you have the right to try and change their minds. If they're saying *really* bad stuff, it's almost your duty. But the key is to do it by starting a debate, not an argument.

It's a big difference. An intelligent, reasoned debate might move thing forwards. It might persuade the person they're wrong. If you charge in, yelling insults from the off, they will just get defensive, double down and slate you back. You'll be one more keyboard warrior, like the ones goading my mate: 'You're a racist!'

'Use your influence to change those who are not like you. That's how we make real change.'

I've learned not to engage with internet trolls. If someone appears on my social media feeds saying 'Oi! Blades! You're a crap presenter in a shit cap! I hate you!', what can I say to *that*? I'm not going to change their mind! So, I don't get into pointless online barnies – but a *conversation*, where I might learn something, is different.

I'm not the most enlightened geezer in the world. Like everybody, I'm shaped by my upbringing. I grew up not knowing any gay people, or non-binary people. I do now, and I respect them and would like to learn more about them. I'm open to being educated, as I am about everything in life.

I mean, I grew up in the seventies and eighties, seeing racist and sexist TV shows like *The Black and White Minstrel Show* and *Love Thy Neighbour*, and comedians laughing at gay people. I see now how wrong those programmes were, but I also know they shaped the attitudes of a lot of people my age and older.

How do we try to educate those guys to have more enlightened attitudes? I know one thing – it's not by shouting 'Idiot!' or 'Bigot!' at them. The trick is to engage with them politely and respectfully. Explain your point of view. *Use your influence to change those that are not like you.*

A lot of people can't be bothered talking to people whose opinions are different from theirs. They prefer just to chat with like-minded souls who think the same way as them. That's all very nice, but the problem is that your social circle turns into an echo chamber. It just reinforces what you already think.

I've never believed in preaching to the converted like that. For me, the life lesson is that it makes a lot more sense to reach out to the people who don't agree with you. It's the only way to try to change their mind – or to give them a chance to try to change yours.

I mean, what is the point of being a vegan and telling a fellow vegan all about the virtues of veganism? *Like, hello?* They know that stuff already! If you are wanting to spread the word about a plant-based diet, you need to engage with the people who don't know about it or might even be opposed to it.

Ideally, a vegan-diet advocate needs to talk to a Texan who keeps his own cows, slaughters one of them at the start of each month and eats rare steak every single day! Because if you can make a few reasonable animal-rights points and get *him* to change his ways, then that is a proper achievement!

Sadly, most people won't want to. They'll take one look at our cow-eating Texan pal's social media and think to themselves, *I don't want to talk to him – he's ignorant!* And, you know what? They may be right – but by writing him off, they're being as ignorant as he is. And nothing changes.

It's as true in real life at it is online. There's no point in just gabbing off about all your opinions to people who already agree with you anyway. That's why, a year or so ago, when *The Sun* newspaper asked me to write an article for them about Black History Month, I jumped at the chance.

I got a load of grief for it, mind you! A lot of people, in the Black community and beyond, were horrified at me for writing for *The Sun*. 'What are you doing dealing with that rag, Jay?' they asked me. 'It's nasty! I wouldn't have it in my house, not even as toilet paper!'

A lot of people in Liverpool were particularly upset at me working with *The Sun* because of the way that paper covered the Hillsborough disaster in 1989, when so many football fans died.

And, believe you me, I don't believe *The Sun* is perfect . . . but I figured I had more to gain from writing for them than to lose.

Think about it! A load of *Sun* readers might not naturally be all that well disposed towards Black History Month, Black Lives Matter, or even Black people as a whole. But if they know me from *The Repair Shop*, read an article by me and think, *Hm, OK, maybe Jay has got a point* . . . what's not to like about that?

As far as I was concerned, even having the article in there in the first place was a little triumph and a bit of progress. Not that long ago, newspapers like *The Sun* would have been saying Black History Month was a waste of time, or taking the piss out of it. Now, there was my piece explaining why we need it! *Bosh!*

I've got no illusions here. I know that reaching out to people who have opposing views to you is a challenging life lesson, and some people find it hard to do. In my own community, there are people who are vehemently opposed to me having any dealings with tabloid newspapers. They think they're evil: beyond hope.

I don't agree with them, but I know why they feel how they do. You look at those papers' front pages sometimes, with their headlines like IMMIGRANTS SWAMP OUR COUNTRY, and you wince. It's particularly damaging since these newspapers are influential. People read the stuff in there and they believe it.

Back in the day, before there was as much integration as we have now, readers used to see the negative things that those papers wrote about Black people and believe them. They might not know any Black people – then they'd meet their first one, maybe at work, and be surprised to find that he was a lovely geezer!

It would puzzle them. 'You're all right for a Black bloke, you are, Trevor!' they'd say. '*You're not like the others.*' And they meant it as a compliment! They didn't know any better but, in a way, they weren't really to blame for their ignorance. They'd been force-fed it by the papers they read on the way to work every day.

Now, that way of thinking is not totally dead. I used to get it when I worked in factories and on building sites – '*You're all right, you are Jay! You're not like the others!*' And now I'm on the telly, I'm sure it still goes on, on a much bigger scale.

I know, for a fact, that there are people who would have crossed the street to avoid me before I got famous, or locked their car doors as I walked past, who will now come running up to me for a chat and a selfie. They may not know any Black people but they love *The Repair Shop*: '*Ah, I like Jay! He's not like the others!*'

And those viewers are friendly, polite and nice to me when we meet. OK, they might not share my background, or my worldview, but they're not going to understand them unless I reach out to them and maybe make them think a little bit. And that means talking to the outlets that they get their news from.

I know a lot of actors and showbiz people won't talk to the *Daily Mail*. They find it quite a toxic, negative publication, and they don't like the attitudes it puts across to its readers. It's a very conservative newspaper that can appear to be resistant to a lot of the changes that we as a society need.

'You achieve so much more by conversation and communication than you do through contempt and confrontation.'

Again, I understand the antipathy towards the *Mail* but I don't agree with it. If I am going to reach out to people who don't agree with me, to try to achieve some real change, well, I need to be talking to the *Daily Mail*'s readers! So, if they ever want to interview me about a new show I'm doing, I always agree to it.

It's that same life lesson again: 'You achieve so much more by conversation and communication than you do through contempt and confrontation.' I would rather work with the *Mail* and reach its readers than reject it. I hope we can get to a better understanding that way, on both sides . . . and I think it's working.

The *Mail* has been good to me in ways it maybe wouldn't have if I didn't talk to them, like those other showbiz people don't. When *Making It* came out, they did an article about my non-dad, The Man Who Contributed Towards My Birth, and the twenty-plus children he has had by countless different women.

Now, I know that piece could easily have been a tabloid hatchet job that implied that TMWCTMB was typical of all Caribbean males . . . but it wasn't. It was a nice, sensitive piece that was sympathetic towards the background I had had, and the way I had turned out.

A Black lawyer friend of mine who doesn't like the *Mail* at all read it, and she was dumbfounded. 'That was a prime opportunity for them to be negative about the Black community, and they didn't do it!' she said. 'They wrote so thoughtfully about you and your situation. What have you *done* to them?'

And what *had* I done to them? Nothing, except reach out to them, give them the time of day, treat them courteously and respectfully, and not write them off. And now they do the same to me. There is a life lesson *there* if ever I saw one.

We all need to do this – talk to people who aren't like us, and who hold different views – because, if we don't do it, society will carry on getting more and more fractured. There are too many people in positions of authority who would like to separate and divide us, and we can't allow that to succeed.

It doesn't matter if you are a Conservative or Labour supporter; if you're Muslim, Hindu or Catholic. For me, we all need to step outside of our little tribes, get together with people from other backgrounds and beliefs, and talk about how we can sort out our differences. *That* is the only way that we're going to be able to move forward.

I'm very lucky that, thanks to *The Repair Shop* and television,

I now have a profile and a platform that enables me to reach out, talk to, and try to influence some of society's proper big decision-makers. And, let's face it, they don't come much more influential or powerful than our monarch, King Charles III!

Actually, I'm getting a bit ahead of myself here. When I first heard from HRH King Charles, he wasn't yet the king: he was still the Prince of Wales. I received a letter from his office a couple of years ago now, asking me if I would be an ambassador for the Prince's Foundation. And it was bang up my street.

The Prince's Foundation is an organization that aims to create communities for a more sustainable world. It offers young people a whole range of education and training programmes, especially in the kind of heritage crafts that are in danger of dying out if we don't train the next generation how to do them.

Boom! I was totally up for this! It just ticks so many of my boxes and what moves me: a love of community, helping young people who might need a leg-up and preserving the kind of heritage crafts that we showcase and put into use on *The Repair Shop* every single week. Yeah! I couldn't wait to get involved.

Well, I couldn't wait to get involved . . . but it took a while to get going. The Prince of Wales invited me to Dumfries House, up in Scotland, where the Foundation is based. In fact, his office asked me up three times, but every time I was mad busy, had a schedule clash and had to decline.

The fourth time I received an invite, I thought, *Hang on, this is crazy! The future king is asking me to drop in to his gaff and I'm saying I haven't got time?! Give yourself a slap, Jay!* So, I cleared a couple of days in my diary and arranged to go to Scotland to see Prince Charles in August 2021.

I was going up on my tod to talk about the Foundation but then the plan changed. A guy at Dumfries House used to work at Ricochet, the production company who make *The Repair Shop*, and he got in touch with his ex-colleagues. 'Jay's coming up here for a chat,' he said. 'Why don't we do a show while he's here?'

Naturally, *The Repair Shop* loved the idea! Prince Charles (as he was then) was up for it, so he dug out a couple of items around the stately home that needed a bit of expert repair – a Victorian vase and an eighteenth-century clock – and I headed off to meet him with Kirsten, Steve and Will from the workshop.

Let me tell you, the producers took it proper seriously! We had to do two full days of rehearsals to pin down exactly what would happen when I met the Prince of Wales – what I had to say, what I could and couldn't do, and the whole etiquette of how you have to behave around royalty. And I have never been so bored in my life!

Like I've already said, I don't like to over-prepare for meeting *Repair Shop* guests. I like to just roll up, open my mouth and have a natural chinwag with them. But I had to spend two days in the workshop 'practising' for the encounter with a guy who was pretending to be Charles.

He was running through everything he thought Charles

might say and the show's producers were suggesting things I might say in reply. I humoured them and played along with it but, if I am honest, after an hour or two I was on autopilot: 'Yes.' 'No.' 'Yeah.' 'Sorry, what?' I can't pretend that I took it very seriously!

Because the truth is, I wasn't at all nervous about meeting Prince Charles. Maybe I *should* have been, but I just wasn't. As I said earlier, I've just always had this crazy level of confidence, or more likely naivety, that lets me waltz into pretty much any situation and not feel awkward. It's just the way I'm built.

I'm still not sure if it's a blessing or a curse that I go through the world like that! If I'm honest, I think it's the former. I've never been impressed or intimidated by celebrity, and I certainly never think of *myself* as a celebrity. That gives me some proper comical moments when I'm out and about.

I'll be walking down the street and someone will say, 'All right, Jay?' I'll stop and say, 'Hello, how're you doing?' Then I'll look at them, realize that I don't know them, and think, *Oh yeah, I'm famous, aren't I? THAT'S how they know me!*

I think there's a good life lesson in there. We live in a celebrity-obsessed world, so it's easy to go a bit radio-rental if you bump into someone famous in the street. But they're just going about their business the same as you are. They're no more special than you. Don't believe all that you read in the gossip mags!

Anyway, the upshot of all this was that when I met the Prince of Wales, walking down the gravel drive outside of Dumfries

House, I wasn't nervous. And the funny thing was, he didn't say one single thing that the actor guy had said in our two-day rehearsals, and nor did I! *I knew it was a waste of time!*

In fact, the first thing that Prince Charles said to me, when we met, was, 'Ah – the wandering furniture-restorer!' And I replied by gesturing at the small set of shears that he was unexpectedly carrying in his hand.

'Hold on a minute, are you on the tools?' I asked him. 'What you got there?'

'Yes, I always take my pruning things wherever I go [*around the estate*],' he told me. 'I always find something to snip, and things that need addressing!'

The prince and I walked and chatted, and I hope this don't sound weird, but it felt like meeting a mate. He's from the royal estate and I'm from a council estate, but we got on great right from the get-go – and the main reason for that was that the two of us have a shared interest. No: a shared *passion*.

HRH King Charles is bang into heritage crafts and his Foundation offers apprenticeships to young people to work with natural materials such as stone, wood, plaster and pigments. Basically, it trains them up to be master craftsmen skilled in holistic, environmentally sustainable crafts. And what's not to like about *that*?

I loved seeing the young people at Dumfries House training in stonemasonry, thatching, blacksmithing and wood carving, among other ancient skills. It was so great to see – they were learning some of the invaluable crafts we put to use on *The Repair Shop* every week, and they were loving every minute of it.

'A great tragedy is the lack of vocational education in schools,' Prince Charles told me. 'Not everybody is designed to be academic . . .'

'Not me!' I agreed.

'But I've seen the difference we can make to people who have technical skills, which we need all the time,' he went on. 'I have the greatest admiration for them. [*Those skills*] are something that have been forgotten.'

As a man who lives for vintage crafts and restoration, it was music to my ears! I saw students making an oak-framed building from scratch. I met a young lady making amazing designs in metal. And I learned how many of the Foundation's budding craftsmen have gone on to have brilliant careers in the outside world, then returned to the Foundation to work as tutors. *Wow!*

Prince Charles made me truly welcome at Dumfries House and he extended the same hospitality when he met *The Repair Shop* team. Kirsten was all ears as he showed her a vase originally made for his great-grandmother, Queen Victoria, that got badly chipped when it fell off a table: 'Nobody owned up!' he laughed.

Steve was perplexed when the prince showed him a carriage clock that had seen better days. 'It's had some very strange things done to it!' he told His Royal Highness. 'I need to get this into the barn to have a look at it!' Will chipped in eagerly, promising to make the clock's case look pukka while Steve fixed its workings.

Our restorers always give a hundred per cent to every damaged item that comes into *The Repair Shop* but they certainly brought their best games to HRH Prince Charles's artefacts! They had them as good as new and gleaming, and when the Prince of Wales came into the workshop to pick them up, he was well impressed.

'Fantastic!' he said, as Steve and Will unveiled the newly restored clock. 'It just shows what all the love and care and attention can do.' He was even more impressed when he heard the timepiece's chimes and bells ringing out again: 'I can't thank you enough!'

The prince was just as fulsome in his praise when he had a butchers at the vase, which Kirsten had restored to its 1897 glory. 'Now, you see, just look at that!' he gasped. 'That is fantastic! How do you do it? I would never have believed it! I'm thrilled, I promise you!' And you know what? He really was. You could tell.

Prince Charles's visit to *The Repair Shop* was a lot of fun but what really excited me – and still does – about the whole palaver was the brilliant work that the Prince's Foundation is doing around heritage crafts and apprenticeships. And the funny thing is that he and I, odd couple that we are, might just keep in touch.

We got on so well when we met that somebody wrote on Twitter, 'Look out, Ant and Dec, there's a new double act in town!' That made me laugh but, also, I think it's a super-crucial life lesson about how two people with nothing in common in their backgrounds or their lives can get on if they share common ideals.

Now that Prince Charles is King Charles III, I think he has a lot of ideas about how he can use the role to improve society. He is interested in Black Lives Matter, which we discussed, and, between you and me, he's even invited me back up to Dumfries House for dinner soon to talk about possible future Foundation projects. And, this time, I won't turn him down three times before I finally go!

What could we work on in future, the king from the royal estate and the boy from the council estate? Who knows? But I'm excited to find out. Watch this space.

I have to say, His Royal Highness has got a hell of a job on! Even with all the confidence that I have, I'm not sure I'd fancy taking on the role of being king! But I'm impressed that, at the head of the country, we have someone who wants to bring about real change and is willing to reach out to people very unlike him to make it happen.

I don't think I'm cut out to be a monarch. We're never gonna see King Jay I, and I think that's probably just as well! But if it ever did happen, in some kind of *Star Trek* parallel universe, I know exactly what I'd do. Again, it's to do with the life lesson that this chapter is all about: 'Use your influence to change those who are not like you. That's how we make real change.'

If I was king, I'd pass a new law that gives everybody in the country a week off work every month. *Wahey! I'd be a well popular king, right?* But you wouldn't be able to spend that week watching TV, or down the pub. You'd have to do something very specific with it.

My law would make everyone spend that week going to a new part of the country to meet people with a totally different background from them. If you're from an inner-city council estate, you'd get to go and live in a tiny village of 500 people in Somerset. You'd have no choice. It'd be mandatory!

'Use your influence to change those who are not like you. That's how we make real change.'

What would you do when you got there? Just *talk*. Talk to the locals about their lives, how they live and how they think. Talk, and *listen*. You may not agree with all they say. It might even get heated! That doesn't matter. You'd go to bed, calm down and the next day you'd talk and listen again.

It wouldn't be like the internet, where everyone turns into keyboard warriors, hurling abuse! You'd sit side-by-side, talk to these people and learn from each other. It would open your eyes. And, after a week, you'd understand each other a million times better. What a great life lesson!

In fact, you know what? It's such a fantastic idea that I might even speak to King Charles and see if he can make it happen . . . lol . . .

9

LOVE

'You may not have tomorrow to say "I love you"'

Back in chapter 7, I was telling you that you have to live each day as if it's your first: wake up and be willing to be a beginner every morning. Well, now I've got some more advice, which might even sound a touch contradictory: you've also got to remember to live each day as if it's your last.

What do I mean by that? I mean that when there's something that you need to deal with in life in order to move forward, whether it's work or in your personal life, you should deal with it there and then. Because if you don't do that, and you keep prevaricating, one day you might really, really regret it.

Don't keep putting things off! You can say 'Oh, I'll do that tomorrow!', but then one day something horrible might happen to you, or to somebody close to you, and then tomorrow isn't going to come. And the most important thing that you should never procrastinate over is telling somebody that you love them.

Some things in life are set in stone and you can't change them. We all lose people sometimes. Loved ones pass on. And the people who find it the hardest to come to terms with their loss are those who never got, or *took*, the chance to tell the person they've lost what they thought of them. To tell them that they loved them.

'I love you.' They're such powerful words, and they can mean so many different things . . . and yet not everybody has the pleasure and the luxury of hearing them as they grow up. I'm one of them. I never had a dad, and the first time my mum ever told me that she loved me, I was forty years old.

It was never said in our house, so the first time my mum said it to me, when I was a fully grown, middle-aged man, it really threw me. I remember thinking, *What?! Oh, shit!* I didn't know what to reply, but I heard myself saying, 'Oh! I. Love. You. Too. Mum!' It was *such* a weird experience – I think for both of us!

Why didn't my mum say it to me, or to my brother, Justin, before then? Was it that she didn't love us, or was it down to the way she was brought up herself? I think it was the latter. Her own mum was a very cold woman and I guess that must have shaped Mum's behaviour, whether she knew it or not.

It meant that when I was a kid, I didn't really understand the *concept* of love. I didn't know what it meant. I understood respect, because Mum drilled that into us, and I understood that she'd always give us food, clean the house around us, and look after us. But . . . *love*? Nah, I just didn't get what that was.

I mean, is your parents caring for you 'love', or is it duty? Are they just fulfilling the role they've been given? Look at nature – most animals look after their young but then, when they're grown, they kick them out and leave them to fend for themselves. I guess when I was a kid, that was how our relationship felt to me.

I'm not trying to slate my mum here. She never said 'I love you' but I reckon she did, in her own way, and she still does. I love her too, and now I'm older, and have more understanding of life and how it works, I can say it to her without feeling weird. But the point I'm making is that 'love' is different for everyone.

It's an important life lesson: there's this idea that family love is universal, and all kids grow up knowing their parents love them to death. But the reality isn't like that. What about all the thousands of kids who grow up in children's homes? Where are *they* supposed to be getting their parental love from?

For me, 'love' is one of the biggest words in the world and it can be one of the most confusing. Some people think it should be like it is in the movies, or in songs: all gazing into one another's eyes, and holding hands, and walking through sunny meadows. We're sold a one-size-fits-all idea of love and a lot of people buy into it.

I never did. As a kid, I used to watch a lot of American TV shows, and when I heard characters saying 'I love you' all the time, it sounded sickly and false, the same as when they said, 'Have a nice day.' It meant nothing to me. I mean, I used to watch *The Waltons*, and life on my estate in Hackney was *nothing* like that!

It's the same as what you hear at music gigs. When pop singers are on stage at the O2, and they tell the crowd, 'I love you!' – do they really? Those 20,000 strangers who they don't know from Adam? To me it just sounds like showbiz gush.

No, the people you love are the ones you hang out with every day. You know you can trust them and they've got your back. As I grew into my teens, I spent all my time playing with my mates and cousins on the estate. We were all proper tight – but I hate to think what might have happened if I'd told them that I loved them!

Well, I know what would have happened – if I'd gone around Hackney telling my mates that I loved them, I wouldn't have had any mates! They'd have thought I was well weird! They'd be having muttered conversations behind my back:

'Bruh, Jay just told me that he loved me!'

'Shut up! Why would he say that?'

'Nah, he did, man! I heard him! And he told me, too!'

'*Shiiiiiit . . .*'

134

I don't know if they'd have beaten me up, but they wouldn't be my friends no more! We all played together, and respected one another, and we'd have fought to the death to defend each other and our patch, but we weren't going around saying 'I love you!' That wasn't how we rolled in the eighties!

Nowadays, kids say it to each other all the time. If you overhear a teenage girl in the street on the phone to her mates, every conversation that she has ends with, 'OK, later! Love you!' Youngsters are programmed by TV and movies and YouTube that that is just what you do. And when I say 'youngsters', I mean *proper* young.

I have a great time talking to my five-year-old niece. I was with her recently, and her grandmother told me, 'Guess what? She's given her phone number to a boy!'

'Really?' I asked my niece, pretending to be shocked. 'Why you done that, then?'

'Oh, I've got a crush on him,' she told me.

'What?' I joked. 'He fell on you and he crushed you?'

'No, Uncle Jay! Not *that* kind of crush!'

'Well, what do you mean, then?'

'A crush means you love somebody,' she told me, patiently. 'So, I gave him my number.'

It was a little nipper explaining to a fifty-year-old what love is. And the funny thing is, she doesn't even have a phone number – she's five years old! She just knows from the TV shows she watches that you 'fall in love' with a boy and then you give him your number. She's starting well early on the life lessons!

Like everything else, your view of love and what it means to you changes as you grow older. You see new depths and angles. Plus, generations change. My mum may not have told me that she loved me until I was well into middle age, but I told my own kids 'I love you' right from when I first had them. Right from the get-go.

I can remember cradling my first son, Levi, a few days after he was born, kissing him, and telling him, 'I love you'. It's something that I wouldn't have been able to imagine myself saying even a month earlier, before I was a dad, but when I held him and whispered it to him, it felt the most natural thing in the world.

It's a funny one, but I think this is a life lesson that you might not really appreciate until you become a parent – and then, you just *get* it. For me, when you have a kid, and you hold him or her, and he or she is *yours*, you get this feeling that you've never, ever felt before. It's overwhelming, and the only word for it is *love*.

It's so strange. You hold this little baby, and your thought process goes something like this: *Wow! Look at you! I'm going to look after you, and protect you, and do all I can to make you happy, and part of that is telling you how I feel about you: I love you!* It's what they call unconditional love. And it's unique.

There is no more fundamental life lesson than this one: you

never stop loving that child for the rest of your life, even if things go wrong between you and their mum, and circumstances pull you apart for a lot longer than you'd like. Mind you, that's not to say that children don't test that unconditional love!

Before you know it, you suddenly find that that child is a teenager and is doing all sorts of shit that you don't think is a good idea. You try to give them some sound advice, and in return you get, 'Oh, jog on, Dad! What do *you* know? You're not living in the modern world!'

Believe you me, you don't feel like turning around then and telling them, 'I love you – unconditionally!' You're more likely to be swearing under your breath about ungrateful little so-and-sos! But that's the way of life. Sometimes, you can't stop them making a mistake. You just have to be there for them afterwards.

What you have to learn as you go through life, I reckon, is that 'love' is an enormous word and it means far more than one thing. Your love for your family and your kids is a very different thing from the love you might feel for friends or even for colleagues. But they're all just as real and just as valid.

I've worked on *The Repair Shop* for six years now and a few of the restorers – Dom and Steve and Kirsten and Will – have been there as long as I have. We've hung out day in, day out and worked and played closely together. Obviously, we have all grown very, very close: a proper little gang.

It's a bit the same as when I was a teenager running with

my mates in Hackney. I didn't tell them that I loved them, and I'm not going to start swanning around the barn declaring it to the repairers now, because that would look *well* peculiar! But at the same time, we all share a trust, and a closeness, that probably *is* some sort of love.

'*You may not have tomorrow to say "I love you".*' It's true, but at the same time, it's possible to show your friends, and work-mates, that you care for them without coming out with something embarrassing. You can show it just by being kind and respectful. And I think we do that in *The Repair Shop*. Every day.

Mind you, I'm sitting here now pontificating about love, and what it all means, yet when you look at the world, it can seem like love is in very short supply! You pick up a newspaper, or you scroll through the headlines on a news website, and you are not filled with warm, mushy feelings.

'You may not have tomorrow to say "I love you".' You read about the war in Ukraine, and the one per cent owning half of the world's wealth while starving people are sleeping on the streets, and if you're not careful you can get very cynical, very quickly. If there's all this love in the world, how did everything get in such a state?

Because the truth is that *the world should not be like this*. There's enough food, enough money, enough resources on the planet that everybody should be able to live in comfort and security. So why do so many political leaders want to divide us all? Why do so many people want to make things harder for others?

The hippies used to think that love can solve all the world's problems. The Beatles came right out and said it: 'All You Need Is Love'. Before I was born, that Sixties generation banged on about peace and love, and said that if we all wore flowers in our hair, everything would be cushty. Or something like that.

How did that work out? Not well! Young people had a lot of bohemian fun and took a lot of drugs and had a lot of sex, but I don't think it made society any better in the long term. All the same inequalities remained. It didn't address any of the serious issues: it was just one big, happy party.

We need more love in the world, sure, but what we need more than that is more *understanding*. That is how we can start getting to grips with global poverty, and people dying of hunger, and the climate crisis. Don't get me wrong, love is great, but it can't do all *that* on its own! No matter what The Beatles said.

To me, it's yet more proof that there are different kinds of love – and as you get older, and more sussed, you learn to differentiate between them. There's love in the abstract sense, and love like you see in movies, and then there's the one that really counts: the love that you have at home, when you get behind closed doors.

And that is the serious stuff. Let's not mess about here! Your relationship with your partner is the most crucial thing in your life, bar none. Let's face it, there's a reason why nearly every movie made, and almost every song written, is about love, or falling in love. It's because that's what we all care about.

You spend every day of your life with your partner. You go to sleep every night with them and you wake up with them every morning. It's a simple fact: if that relationship is not a good one, you will *not* be happy in your daily life. And yet it is so easy, and there are so many ways, to cock it up.

When you're a teenager, you absorb all the romantic fictions you're fed by movies and songs and you think your own life has to be like that. You meet your first partner and you fling the L-word about all the time: 'I love you!' You get carried away and you can easily end up getting married and having kids way too young.

I guess I was like that when I met Maria, my first serious girlfriend, in my teens. It was exciting, sure, all passion and hot tempers and falling out and making up, and we loved each other in a very adolescent way. It was always going to end up how it did: with me being a dad, just out of my teens, to Levi.

It was passionate love but it wasn't stable and it didn't last. I have to admit, that was a bit of a theme in my early life. I had a lot of love affairs and relationships – and another son, Dior – in my twenties. I was into my partners at the time, and what we felt *was* love, in a way, but, looking back, none of the relationships were built to last. I wasn't ready.

Well, one good thing about relationships is that you learn as you go along. You pick up more life lessons about love as you grow older than any other topic. And you get tired of the rows, and the tensions, and the drama. 'No More Drama' as Mary J. Blige said! You want to be in a partnership that has love, but that is also solid, and is one that you can trust.

I've been through the pain of break-ups and of divorce and I don't want ever to go through them again. When I met the beautiful woman who I'm married to today, Lisa, I fell head-over-heels in love and I knew that it was special pretty quickly. But I also knew to be careful not to repeat my previous mistakes.

I met Lisa in quite a weird way: through an online exercise class during the first Covid lockdown! Lisa is a fitness instructor, and she and I really hit it off when I joined her class. When we met up in real life, we had proper chemistry – and the great thing was that we went into our relationship with our eyes wide open.

I didn't find it hard to tell Lisa 'I love you' because it is true – but at the same time, she and I both know that those little words don't solve everything. They're not a magic spell to make everything hunky-dory. The only way to do that is to work hard at your relationship, together, through the good times and the bad.

There's the life lesson. You've got to become a unit, a unity, and to do that, you have to respect one another. You have to respect each other's personalities and differences, especially if, like me and Lisa, you come from completely different back-grounds and histories to each other.

We all go through life with our baggage and the complexes that we have picked up along the way. Some of it you learn to jettison as you go: some of it stays with you for ever, no matter what you do. It means that you can be touchy and sometimes a word from your partner can trigger you, even if they don't mean it to.

When that happens, it's easy to fly off the handle – especially if that is what you've always done before! But the key is not to do that but to explain, carefully, what has hurt you: 'What you said upset me because of *this*.' Then you can talk it out in a respectful way. You can still be that unit; that *unity*.

Of course, one reason that relationships fail in our younger years, is the old 'wandering eye'. It's often men who succumb to this – it's just how we're built. I confessed in *Making It* to having an eye for the ladies, and it hasn't half brought me some grief over the years! Seriously!

Thankfully, my running around and cheating is well behind me now, and I couldn't be happier or more relieved about it. As you get older, you don't want to behave like that. You want to respect your partner and your relationship. I still love to see an attractive woman – and, luckily, I'm married to the most attractive one I know!

At the risk of embarrassing my good lady wife, I find her incredibly sexy. I have photos of her on my phone (no, not *those* kinds of photos!) and I sneak a look at them several times every single day. I'm happy to admit it! I have a good look at my phone, and I love what I see.

When you are young and stupid, you think that fancying someone is all there is to love. It's not, of course, but it's still important. The brilliant thing is that beauty is in the eye of the beholder, so I will never stop fancying Lisa as we grow old together. It's a win–win situation!

If you think that love is like it is in the movies, a big romantic fiction, it's too easy to give up on the days that it doesn't measure up. Too easy to think, *Sod this, this isn't what I signed up for!* and check out. It doesn't match up to the unrealistic image in your mind, and so you bail out and do a runner.

Imagine if you went on a holiday to Barbados, expecting brilliant sunshine every day, and one morning it was cold and raining. You might want to get on the next plane and get out of there! But love isn't like that. Love is sticking it out, working at it, and waiting for the sun to come out again. Because it will.

To get back to the lesson that I started this chapter with: real love needs hard work, and it is about dealing with any issues you have to deal with, together, as soon as they come up. It's about not putting them off until tomorrow. And it's about never, ever, leaving it too late to say 'I love you'.

And you know what? Learn this life lesson well, and follow it closely, and you might just end up being very, very happy for the rest of your life. I really can't recommend it enough . . .

10

PUT IT ALL TOGETHER . . .

*'We should give meaning to life,
not wait for life to give us meaning'*

Early on in this book, I explained that it is divided into ten sections, but all of the life lessons overlap. They dovetail and intertwine into what I suppose we can call my philosophy of life (don't forget, I *am* a former philosophy student!). And, for me, this is the saying that sums it all up. In fact, I'll say it again: 'We should give meaning to life, not wait for life to give us meaning.'

Bosh! For me, that is what it all comes down to. What all these words amount to. We are all lucky enough to be alive, so we have to go out there and live our lives to the full. Experience as much as we can. Because life is not going to give you meaning on its own. It's down to you to find it. To create it.

I didn't exactly learn Latin at my secondary school – let's face it, they hardly taught me bloody English! But one Latin phrase that I do know is *carpe diem*: seize the day. It means you have to treat life like a great big exciting adventure, and leap into every new experience you can, and it's a saying that suits me to a T.

I talked earlier about sometimes turning your head to look out of a different window so you can see new vistas and

'We should give meaning to life, not wait for life to give us meaning.'

possibilities, and that is what you have to try to do every day of your life. See as much as you can; *do* as much as you can. Life isn't going to have much meaning if you just sit in your comfort zone.

How can I put it as plainly as possible? Basically: if you're in doubt about doing a new thing, forget your apprehension and fears and give it a go. Jump right in! In my life, I've definitely been naive going into loads of new situations, but I see that as a strength, not a weakness. Because they've *nearly* all worked out.

It's very easy to be passive in life and just do what you know. To *let life happen to you*, rather than be active and creative. And I understand why a lot of people sit and let things happen rather than firing the starting gun themselves. But, believe me, you'll be a lot more excited every day if you shape your own future.

Did someone mention starting guns? Well, let's look at Usain

Bolt again. He could crouch on his starting blocks, wait for the pistol to go off – *BANG!* – and then do the same thing he always did: belt around that track like greased lightning and win the race. But his work really started *way* before that pistol got fired.

Usain had to spend days, weeks, months, *years* getting ready for that moment. He had to get up early every morning, eat all the right food and, mainly, train and train and train like crazy. He had to do everything right. Doing that gave meaning and purpose to his life. He didn't just let life happen to him.

I know some people might say that Usain was lucky. He was incredibly talented, sure, but he also knew exactly what he wanted to do with his life: he wanted to be the fastest man alive. He had a mission. Whereas thousands of people – and maybe you? – wake up each day without a clue what they want to do or be.

Well, you know what's cool about that? If you don't know what you want to do, then everything is possible! It's like you're at a crossroads on a road, not knowing which way to go. It means whichever way you turn will be into the unknown, an adventure. And if you don't like it? Just take another route instead!

Or maybe you think from an early age that you want to be, say, an accountant. You study hard, pass all the exams, get a job – and then you hate the day-to-day routine and don't like your clients. Well, you've had an experience and learned from it. And never forget, you can always jack it in and do something else instead.

I mean, I knew as a kid I wanted to do great things – I just hadn't got a Scooby what they would be! I wasn't pulled in any one direction. There were definitely points in my twenties when I was pretty aimless: doing labouring and factory and construction work because it was all I knew, and I thought it was all I could do.

I don't look down on those times and those jobs. *Never!* They were all experiences, and I learned things from them, and probably my focus in those days was more on spending the money they earned me and enjoying myself in my spare time. But the jobs themselves were not what you might call fulfilling.

I needed that fulfilment, and I found it by naively throwing myself into a line of work that I knew nothing about: volunteering and working with people in need. I did my stint at the Cyrenians homeless hostel, and I worked with young delinquents and with people with mental health issues, and it was a revelation for me.

In society, what we're always told is: work hard at school, get your GCSEs, get a good job, a partner, a nice house, two-point-five kids. Volunteering showed me my life didn't *have* to be like that! I could find a different, satisfying way to live – and the funny thing was, I did it by making it up as I went along!

There was no map, no plan, that took me from building sites to volunteering to university to community work to running a charity to TV presenting. But all those things happened because

I kept throwing myself whole-heartedly into fresh experiences. Having new adventures. And, somehow, it all worked out.

'Life is not a problem to be solved, but a reality to be experienced.'

When I was a kid, I used to watch an American TV programme called *Highway to Heaven*. It starred Michael Landon, who used to be the dad in *Little House on the Prairie*, and it was about an angel who is sent down to Earth to wander from town to town, helping people in need.

Now, you might laugh at this one, but when I watched it, I used to think that that was how *I'd* like to live! I've never been an angel – let's face it, I've been more of a devil, at times! – but I loved the idea of spending life roaming from place to place, doing good deeds, with no two days ever the same.

There's another phrase I'd like to hit you with: 'Life is not a problem to be solved, but a reality to be experienced.' And, if you ask me, if you go from day to day bearing that one in mind, you won't go too far wrong.

What does it mean? It's another way of saying there is no one correct way to live life. It's not a puzzle, that you have to ponder over until you crack it and find the right answer: 'Ah, *that's* the meaning of life!' Don't go asking Alexa, 'What is the meaning of life?' You might as well inquire, 'Alexa, how long is a piece of string?'

No, the only meaning of life that matters is the one that has meaning for you. It may take a while to find it, but you get there by opening yourself up to as many different experiences as possible, and seeing which ones work for you. Whatever floats your boat and makes you happy: *that's* your meaning of life.

You may struggle to get on board with this idea, but every experience that you have in your life benefits you. Every. Single. One. Even bad things like messing up a job, or getting divorced, develop you in the long run: you learn things from those experiences. Even if it's that you'll take care never to do them again.

'If the grass looks greener on the other side, start watering the grass you're on.'

You need to discover what works for you in your work life and, nearer to home, you need to learn how to be happy in relationships and your personal life. And, guess what? This brings me to another little saying that can teach us a lot: 'If the grass looks greener on the other side, start watering the grass you're on.'

That one's well Confucius! If you're of a certain vintage, like me, you might read it and start getting flashbacks to David Carradine in that old TV show, *Kung Fu*: '*Ah, Grasshopper!*' Carradine was a Shaolin monk, Kwai Chang Caine, who used to wander from town to town, dispensing justice and wisdom as he went.

Well, I think even Kwai Chang Caine would be proud of that

saying, because it's a belter! And what it means is this: if you're in a relationship, say, that feels like it's going nowhere and might be running out of time, don't automatically head for the hills. Instead, try to make it work. Talk to your partner. *Communicate*.

Because you might feel as if the two of you are stuck in a desert, with no signs of life, but nothing will grow unless you start to water the ground you are standing on. *How* do you water it? Through communication, and through understanding, and compromise, and love. And then, who *knows* what might spring up?

Like I said in the previous chapter, I used not to be too handy with a watering-can! If it was looking a bit dry around us, I'd be legging it out of there, scanning the horizon for a new girl and some grass that looked a bit greener. Now I'm with Lisa, we water the grass we live on, and you know what? It's coming up just lovely!

In any case, in a wider sense, it's not a good way to live to always be thinking that the grass is greener on the other side. Believe me, there is nothing healthy about that state of mind. If you're always ogling what other people have got, or what you *think* they've got, you're going to end up bitter and envious.

It's not totally your fault if you do that. It's easy to see how it happens. Society pushes us that way. As I said earlier, it can be hard to look at certain people's social media streams and how they portray their life, and not feel well jealous:

God, look at him! His teeth are so straight, and that is the perfect six-pack! If I go to the gym every day, I'll still never get that! His house is amazing – well, it's not a house, it's a palace! His wife is a supermodel – and is that a brand-new, top-of-the-range Lamborghini? Shit, man, why isn't my life like that?

Well, two points here. One, there is no point at all in feeling jealous of what this guy has achieved: he's worked for it, so good luck to him. And two, who's to say his life *is* like that anyway? He's not going to show us the days he's got a paunch and a hangover, has had a barney with his missus, and is kipping on the sofa!

Even so, social media is a powerful force and it's hard not to gawp, even when it is bombarding us with images that make us feel useless by comparison, as if we've achieved nothing in our own lives. Two or three years ago, I was finding that very thing happening to me, and I decided that I had to do something about it.

I was following some very successful people – mentioning no names, but TV presenters, and British actors who've gone over and done well in Hollywood – and they were making me feel well inadequate. I'd look at their glamorous lifestyles, and non-stop exotic holidays, and it made me think that I was a total loser.

I could see how ridiculous it was: I was on TV myself by then, on *The Repair Shop*, and not doing too shabbily, all things considered. I had no reason at all to complain, but their social media output was making me feel as if I was missing out. And I sorted that out by doing the obvious thing.

Which was what? I stopped following them! I didn't make a big deal about it and I didn't have a thing against those guys personally: I still bump into them, now and then, at awards shows and the like, and we have a bit of banter. But their social media wasn't doing it for me, so I logged off.

I'd tell everyone to do the same. It's a strong life lesson worth learning: if you're not enjoying following someone on social media, just stop following them. And that includes me! I try to make my own socials inspirational and inclusive and not boastful, but only follow me if you enjoy them. If you don't, I won't mind.

Basically, if you bumped into somebody in real life and all they did was brag about how big their house is, how flashy their car is, and how many holidays they have a year, you'd soon give them a swerve! Well, do the same thing online. Hang out with the people you like, and who lift you up. Social media is meant to be *fun*.

Right at the start of this book, in the very first chapter, I talked about staying on top of your past so you can have a better view of your future. Well, now we are nearly at the end, I want to revisit that idea with a little bit of a twist: whatever you do, make sure your past doesn't stay on top of *you*.

As the years go by, you come to terms with your past. However hard it may have been, you get to understand it, appreciate it, and, eventually, feel grateful for it: after all, it got you to where you are today! But, sometimes, something will happen and, out of the blue, it drops you right back into a dark place.

The other evening, I was just hanging out in my garden at home, minding my own business. I heard a voice: 'Oi, Jay!' I spun around, looked about me, and there was nobody in sight. And my mind suddenly went racing back to a traumatic incident that happened to me nearly forty years earlier.

When I was a teenager in Hackney, being out and about on the streets could be a dangerous business for me. It wasn't just the racism. By one means or another, I had got myself a bit of a reputation, and plenty of people would have liked to do me harm, given half a chance. I had to always have my wits about me.

One evening when I was fourteen, a mate and I had dropped two girls we knew off at Dalston Junction station. It's normally a busy, bustling part of east London, but that dusk there was nobody about at all. Which made it even scarier when we suddenly heard a loud shout: 'Oi, Blades! Come here!'

We swivelled around quickly but we couldn't see a soul! What I knew, for a stone-cold fact, was that anyone spotting me and yelling after me like that would *not* be good news! My heart was thudding against my chest as my mate and I took off like rockets and sprinted the mile home through the gloom. We didn't stop until we were safely indoors.

That incident freaked us out so much that we didn't even talk to each other about it for the next three days. And now, suddenly, four decades later, a random shout, one evening in Wolverhampton, had catapulted me back four decades to that feeling of sheer terror.

Shit! Who is it? Where is he? What does he want?

Lisa came out in the garden and saw me standing there, all twitchy, with my eyes like saucers. She could tell straight off that something was wrong so she came right over to me. 'What's the matter, Jay?' she asked me. 'What is it?'

'Someone just bloody shouted at me! And I can't see where he is! Who is it?'

'So what? What's the problem?'

'*What's the problem?!*'

And then I realized . . . Lisa didn't have a clue why I was so freaked out. She had no idea why I was frightened out of my wits. So, I took a deep breath and I told her: how shit-scared I had been forty years ago, when I thought I was about to get a kicking, and how this sudden yell had triggered me in exactly the same way.

Lisa listened. She didn't laugh at me, or ask, 'What you on about, you muppet?' She understood. *She got it.* She gave me a hug, and she explained how I had to overcome my instinct-ive terrified reaction, no matter how deeply ingrained in me it may be.

'Your life is very different now from forty years ago, Jay,' she said. 'Nobody is out to get you. You've got to realize that shout probably wasn't anything negative. It was likely that somebody going past recognized you from the telly. You can get rid of that fear now. You don't need it.'

It was total common sense and it was exactly what I had to hear. And there's a key life lesson. If your past suddenly rears up and spooks you out, *talk about it. Communicate.* Don't be embarrassed to share your vulnerabilities with a loved one. Because that is when they can help you to overcome them.

Of course, even if you follow that advice, and even if you absorb and act on every single lesson in this book, you will still feel unhappy sometimes. That's just human nature and the way that life is. And when that happens, don't be hard on yourself. Just bear in mind the next saying I've got for you:

'When the going gets tough, when we're feeling utterly down and discouraged, we need to remember to accept what is, let go of what was, and have faith in the road ahead.'

We're not perfect. Life isn't perfect. There are times it all gets too much. I've been there: driving down that motorway, in the dead of night, looking for a motorway bridge to crash into and end it all. It's easy to get into that bad place where you can't see tomorrow. But, believe me: there is *always* a way out.

You have to *trust the process of life.* Believe in the possibility of a better future. Even if you are temporarily lacking the vision to see that future, you have to trust that it is there, and that things will get better. And don't ever be afraid of asking for the help you need to regain that vision.

If you're lucky, you will have a partner, or somebody close enough for you to turn to, to help you through. And even if you are totally on your own, just think of the times in the past when you've felt the same: that everything is crap and there's no point in going on. Because there is *always* a point.

You turned it around then. You can do it again.

Staying with the theme of this final chapter, that you should give meaning to life, not wait for it to give you meaning, I want to quote some back-up evidence from an inspirational guy who did OK for himself! It's the former US President Barack Obama, who had this to say:

'Change will not come if we wait for some other person, or if we wait for some other time. We are the ones we've been waiting for; we are the change that we seek.'

It's a weird one. When Obama was voted in as president, I wasn't as buzzed about it as some people around me. Obviously, I knew it was a great achievement for him to be the first Black president of the USA. But I didn't want to see him as an amazing exception. I wanted to see him as encouragement that we can *all* do great things.

You see, as far as I'm concerned, *everybody* has that Obama spirit, or that Nelson Mandela spirit, or that Martin Luther King spirit, inside them. If they look deep enough, everyone has the ability to change society. But most people cop out and leave it to others to try to do that. Why? Because they feel powerless.

Look at the big picture! We read all about the one per cent of the population of the world who own the wealth, the big companies, and exert their influence on all the rest of us for how we should live, what we should eat, what we should watch, etc. Well, this is the question that comes up in my mind:

If those one-per-centers control everything, what are the other ninety-nine per cent doing?

Basically, they – we – are giving up, because society has told us you need money and influence if you want to change anything. But that's not true! Real change comes from the bottom: from like-minded people coming together and looking to start some real change. *Then* we might see some ructions!

If just five per cent of the population of the world were to gather together as a community, they could really make some change for the better. 'Yes, we can!' as Obama said. I may see it in my lifetime, I may not. Everybody has the ability to change the world. It's just that so many people choose not to.

I don't want to get too heavy here as we near the end of this book. And I'm not trying to start a revolution – honest! I just want to focus our minds on another little saying I posted on my socials a while ago. This was it: 'When all is said and done, will you have said more than you've done?'

I think this one's pretty self-explanatory, don't you? I'm a big believer in action. In doing stuff. There's no point in just *talking* a good fight. Plenty of people do that, from the comfort of their armchairs. And, when it comes down to it, that doesn't achieve a fat lot.

Life is short. One minute you're a kid, running around and getting into wild scrapes. Then suddenly, before you know it, you're an oldie who

'**When all is said and done, will you have said more than you've done?**'

can hardly run for a bus! Time is precious, and it goes so quickly. You don't want to waste it. *Carpe diem.*

Without meaning to be overly morbid, when you're lying on your deathbed, you don't want to be thinking about all the things that you *didn't* do! You don't want to be ruing the times you copped out. No: you want to know that you gave life your best shot, you gave it meaning, and it made you happy.

Sometimes, I look back at my life to date and I feel a bit flummoxed. How has that troubled, angry kid who left school at sixteen without a single qualification and not even able to read, ended up *here*?

Well, it's been partly down to naivety, and always being willing to give things a go, but mostly it's been because of people I've met who saw something in me that I didn't even see in myself and took a chance on me. The people who saw that I was willing to learn, even when I didn't know what the lesson was!

There are always lessons, all around us and, as I said right at the start of this book, a day that you don't learn something is a wasted day. You want one last life lesson? 'Don't take anything for granted!' I have a career as a TV presenter now, and I feel lucky and grateful for it, but I know I could lose it in a heartbeat.

'Don't take anything for granted!'

How's that, Jay? Well, we live in a cancel culture. I do my best not to say anything that might hurt or offend anyone, but you know what? We all make mistakes. It only takes one loose word, or misplaced comment, from me and I could be wiped off the map. I'd soon be forgotten, just one more pub-quiz question:

What was the name of the flat-cap-wearing presenter of BBC1's The Repair Shop, *who was disgraced and never heard from again?*

Fingers crossed that never happens!

So, if you were to take just one life lesson out of this little book, what should it be? I'd say: 'Always believe in yourself.' If I've got one strength, I think it's that I've never stopped doing that, even

'Always believe in yourself.'

at my lowest points. I've held on to my belief, and it's carried me through. I've said this many times before, and I'll say it again:

If I can do it, anybody can.